PRAISE FOR *BY BREAD ALONE*

By Bread Alone is a soulful, searching glimpse into trusting the goodness of God when it seems most opaque. Kendall Vanderslice trades toxic positivity for the promise of sustenance, and the result is deeply honest and curiously comforting. These pages are dusted with the flour of daily bread. If you are lost, longing, hope-weary, or barely hanging on (aren't we all?), read this and be nourished.

SHANNAN MARTIN
Author of *Start with Hello* and *The Ministry of Ordinary Places*

I am grateful for Kendall Vanderslice's *By Bread Alone*—a sustenance of hope, a needed nourishment for us hungering to create beauty faced with the bitter gaps of our divided cultures. Her words give rise to our tenderness, and her memorable chapters fill our hearts with compassion. Every page of this book (full of recipes) is brimming with refractive colors shining through the broken prisms of her life, a communion journey of service in tears, as a sojourner baker, a fellow maker into the aroma of the new.

MAKOTO FUJIMURA
Artist and author of *Art + Faith: A Theology of Making*

In this deeply personal account, baker-theologian Kendall Vanderslice explores how baking bread can become a lens through which we understand the Eucharist anew and what it means to allow God to form our lives into a living sacrifice for the life of the world. Be moved, touched, and inspired as you journey with Kendall into the world of artisan bread, embodiment, and what it means to fully embrace your vocation.

GISELA KREGLINGER, PHD
Author of *The Spirituality of Wine* and *The Soul of Wine*

By Bread Alone provides a refreshing perspective on the intersection between faith and food. Kendall eloquently uses her baking expertise and experience to poignantly remind us that the simple acts of making, breaking, and eating bread have profound theological implications.

ADRIAN MILLER
James Beard Award winner and executive director of the Colorado Council of Churches

By Bread Alone is a powerful invitation into the rhythms of baking and the rhythms of faith. As Kendall explains, these are complex journeys of nuance and transformation that mirror each other. Through a robust exploration of breadmaking and her own story, Kendall vulnerably and insightfully offers an alternative to the "Wonder Bread theology" that often plagues the church. This book nourishes and satisfies our deepest longings for the Bread of Life.

KAT ARMAS
Author of *Abuelita Faith* and host of *The Protagonistas* podcast

By Bread Alone is a tender and vulnerable story of Kendall's search to be satisfied by God's provision for her given life. A memoir about what it means to be hungry, what it means to be filled, and what it means to not always get what you desire. I loved this book and needed it myself. Every woman who has struggled to love and learn and lean into their body while still looking with hope toward their resurrected body needs this book.

LORE FERGUSON WILBERT
Author of *A Curious Faith* and *Handle with Care*

B

Y

B

R

E

A

D

A

L

O

N

E

BY BREAD ALONE

*A Baker's Reflections on
Hunger, Longing, and the Goodness of God*

KENDALL VANDERSLICE

TYNDALE
MOMENTUM®

A Tyndale nonfiction imprint

Visit Tyndale online at tyndale.com.

Visit Tyndale Momentum online at tyndalemomentum.com.

Visit the author at kendallvanderslice.com.

Tyndale, Tyndale's quill logo, *Tyndale Momentum*, and the Tyndale Momentum logo are registered trademarks of Tyndale House Ministries. Tyndale Momentum is a nonfiction imprint of Tyndale House Publishers, Carol Stream, Illinois.

By Bread Alone: A Baker's Reflections on Hunger, Longing, and the Goodness of God

Designed by Libby Dykstra and Julie Chen

The author is represented by Alive Literary Agency, www.aliveliterary.com.

For information about special discounts for bulk purchases, please contact Tyndale House Publishers at csresponse@tyndale.com, or call 1-855-277-9400.

Library of Congress Cataloging-in-Publication Data

A catalog record for this book is available from the Library of Congress.

ISBN 978-1-4964-6134-6

Printed in the United States of America

29	28	27	26	25	24	23
7	6	5	4	3	2	1

In memory of Rev. Dr. Charles "Big Daddy" Vanderslice,
who modeled deep love for God, passion for education,
and abounding grace for everyone. I only wish you
could have read this book before you went home.

CONTENTS

AUTHOR'S NOTE

This is the story of a baker who can only understand her vocation in light of the story of God's Church through history and around the world. It contains my own perspective on events that intersect with the stories of many others. While I seek to tell my journey with dignity and truth, turning it over and over again to see fractals of God's work throughout, I am limited by the bounds of my own experience and memory. I do not seek to paint any church or community as perfect, nor any community as void of good. I hope that as I share my story, both the places of healing and the places of pain, you find the tools necessary to see God's presence in your own story too.

This book contains discussions of disordered eating, depression, and death. Reader discretion is advised. Some names have been changed and characters merged for privacy and ease of storytelling.

FOREWORD

In her preface to this superb book, Kendall Vanderslice wrote a very simple sentence that triggered an epiphany for me: "As soon as flour hits water, a series of transformations begins." And there it is, the essence of this book, the answer to the question I get asked more than any other: "Why bread?" The answer, if one may be so bold as to say there actually is a definitive answer, begins with that crucial word *transformation*. It is a word, like bread itself, worth peeling back to explore in its many layers, which is what Kendall does. In that sense, this book is a revelation, I would say, of why bread is the most iconic transformational food. Bread, as you will soon see, is a portal that can take us into the depths of what transformation means, what it actually is.

I've been obsessed with this notion of bread as the ultimate transformational food for many years now, so when I talk or write about it, I start with a basic, self-coined definition: transformation means a radical change from one thing into something totally other. I hadn't even looked the word up in the dictionary—my definition just seemed so intuitively obvious. But for the sake of this foreword, I opened my Webster's to *transformation*. Nestled between a number of useless, redundant definitions ("the state of being transformed"), I found this gem: "A change in form, appearance, condition, nature, or character." One word directly above it on the dictionary page, I saw listed *transform*, which included the following: "to change into another substance; to transmute." Full disclosure: I like my definition better, but any and all of these Webster's versions will do for what I'm about to say.

As a baker, teacher, and author of ten bread books, I always frame the process in terms of another definition I coined: the baker's mission is to evoke the full potential of flavor trapped in the grain. It is as simple as that—the baker who evokes the best flavor wins. To accomplish this, one must employ all the tools of his or her craft in order to transform flour, water, salt, and yeast into something totally other; to change it in form, appearance, condition, nature, and character; to change it into another substance; to effect a transmutation.

But here's the twist, as Edward Espe Brown put it when he contributed to the jacket of my first book back in 1991. At the time, he was a baker and already the author of *The Tassajara Bread Book*. He put it with perfect symmetry and elegance: "The baker makes the bread, the making of the bread transforms the baker."

Which brings us back to Kendall Vanderslice and her aha-inducing insight that "as soon as flour hits water, a series of transformations begins." This book, which is both a series of meditations and a collection of touching stories about her own journey of self-discovery, perfectly captures the symbiotic back-and-forth of how the baker and the making of the bread transform each other. Her unique confluence of life experiences, including her literary and theological training, has inspired Kendall to invoke beautifully crafted words that evoke this fascinating mystery. How does transformation occur? Read on to find out.

Peter Reinhart
Charlotte, North Carolina

PREFACE

I was five years old when I stole my first Communion.

Our church, Richardson Heights Baptist, was celebrating its fortieth anniversary. We were meeting in a local high school auditorium to accommodate all the members and guests who had come to mark the occasion. For us, it was a family celebration as much as a church party—marking forty years since my grandparents had married just a month before planting the church.

At the service, attendees overflowed the seating in the auditorium. As a result, my siblings and cousins and I sat in the aisle, next to a box of "Communion to go" cups—shots of grape juice with a cracker attached at the top, all sealed together with plastic. This wasn't the usual manner by which our church remembered Jesus' death and resurrection—it was just a convenient method for this celebration.

I'd watched my parents take Communion dozens of times before, each month when the elders passed silver platters of oyster crackers and tiny cups of grape juice down each pew. They'd eat their share discreetly before bowing in prayer.

"We're thanking God for sending his Son to die for our sins," they whispered to my brother, Davis; my sister, Alyssa; and me, encouraging us to mirror their solemn posture.

Our tradition allowed children to take part in Communion once they could articulate its meaning. Every so often, during our family prayer time on Sunday nights, we'd talk about the forgiveness of sins, about asking Jesus into our hearts, about baptism—an outward expression of inward cleansing. My parents prayed that God would prompt us to utter the words of the Sinner's Prayer whenever our hearts were ready.

At five, I hadn't asked Jesus into my heart yet, and I'd never eaten the cracker or the juice either. But that day the box of Jesus' Body and Blood beckoned. I couldn't pay attention to the sermon, my gaze bouncing between the cardboard container and the preacher onstage.

The low lighting masked my movements, and everyone else's eyes were fixed on the pastor. So I slipped my hand through a slit at the top of the box of Communion cups, and I stole a portion for myself. I peeled back the packaging, careful not to make any noise that might alert my parents to my theft, and I placed the cracker on my tongue. The salty Body stung at first, before it softened inside my mouth. I feared chewing might be too loud, so I savored the taste until Jesus disintegrated on his own. Then I looked at the juice, the cup of forgiveness, and couldn't bear to go on, filled with guilt over the hunger I could not control.

Later that afternoon, I brought the juice container to my parents' room. Sitting on the bench at the end of their bed, I sobbed as I confessed what I'd done.

"I wanted to taste it," I said. "But I didn't drink the juice."

"Do you remember why we take Communion?" Dad asked, kneeling in front of me. Mom sat to my right, holding my trembling hand.

I nodded, then whispered, "Because Jesus died for our sins."

Dad took the cup and looked into my eyes. "Jesus loves you very much," he said. "And he's proud of you for being honest with us."

I smiled, my cheeks stained with tears.

"Can we pray together?" he asked.

The three of us bowed our heads and closed our eyes.

"Jesus, thank you for Kendall's tender heart," Dad said. "For her honesty and her desire to please you. Help her to know how much you love her. Amen."

As we opened our eyes, he pulled the lid off of the juice. "Would you like to drink it?" he asked. My puffy eyes grew wide before I nodded, taking the cup and sipping down the syrupy-sweet Blood.

Two more years passed before I prayed the prayer and was baptized, dunked by my dad in the baptismal pool behind the church stage.

More than two decades have gone by now, but I'm still learning what that meal—the Bread, the Body—means.

———

Bread is central to the story of God's work in the world.

Since the dawn of agriculture, writes bread historian William Rubel, bread has served as a simultaneous blessing and curse.[1] The labor required to plant, harvest, thresh, grind, knead, shape, and bake a loaf reflects the Curse spoken over the soil in Genesis 3. At the same time, bread has served as the core of the human diet in almost all cultures throughout history.

In Scripture, bread functions as a sign of God's presence: the twelve loaves of showbread placed in the Tabernacle (Leviticus 24:5-9) and the bread broken with the disciples on the path to Emmaus (Luke 24:13-33). Bread also exemplifies God's provision, from the manna in the desert (Exodus 16) to the miraculous multiplication of the five loaves (Mark 6:34-44). It serves as a reminder of God's promise of deliverance from the oppression and brokenness of this world: the unleavened bread at Passover (Exodus 12:1-28) and the bread offered by Jesus in the Last Supper (Matthew 26:17-29).

Throughout the history of the Church, Christians have told the story of Christ's death and resurrection through the breaking of bread. While the type of bread used in Communion has been contested (Should it be leavened or unleavened? Must it be made of wheat?), the belief that the element must be recognized as bread has held steady. But the significance of bread goes beyond church walls; it has also been the primary food in the diet of most humans throughout history. Bread is magnificent in both its mundane nature and its absolute necessity.

At the cusp of the twentieth century, new technology emerged in the United States that promised to transform the process of baking bread. For generations, bread making had been the purview of home cooks, typically women, made through unstandardized techniques passed down from generation to generation. But through the concerted effort of marketers and business owners, bread became the domain of professional bakeries that operated with scientific precision.[2]

Until that point, middle-class American consumers had been wary of bread sold in bakeries and stores, where they feared the loaves might be filled with sawdust or chalk to stretch the flour further.[3] Whether or not these fears were warranted, they were amplified during the turn of the century, as changing racial and class demographics threatened to upset the white middle-class status quo.

Thanks to a growing awareness of bacteria—and a pandemic that spread rapidly in urban areas—white consumers masked their fear of change behind a fear of contagion, a convenient shield against immigrants, whom they perceived as dirty and poor. Since most bakeries were run by immigrants, many white consumers decided the only way to ensure a safe diet was to bake bread oneself, at home.[4]

With the invention of industrial baking equipment, commercial bakeries were able to exponentially increase the amount of bread that could be produced in a day. Unlike homemade bread, which was subject to the whims of yeast and the weather, these commercial loaves were soft, uniform, sliced, and white. After taming the living organisms that turn flour into bread, these mechanized bakeries could produce a loaf never touched by human hands.

To convince housewives to let go of the practice of making homemade bread, commercial bakers preyed on their anxieties, advertising the whiteness, cleanliness, and purity of their loaves. They sanitized wild microbes and yeasts to promise consumers a safe, clean loaf.[5]

In reality, the reactions that allow for a bleached-white bread degrade the texture of dough, limit the nutritional value, and hinder the development of flavor. As scientists have discovered in the years since these mass-marketed loaves flooded our grocery aisles, the process impacts the digestibility of bread as well. This "Wonder Bread" offered uniformity and the illusion of safety while transforming consumers' expectations of what bread should be.

Fears of contamination proliferated in sacramental practice as well. Until the discovery of germ theory, Christians of all traditions practiced Communion using a common cup and, for many, a common loaf. Although Catholic, Orthodox, and Protestant Christians clung to different convictions about how the element ought to be prepared and received, they were united in their use of a shared chalice.[6] With increasing scientific understanding about the spread of disease came pressure for clergy to reform these liturgical norms, whether by restricting the cup to the clergy alone, as Catholics had done for centuries, or by offering individual portions to church members in small plastic cups.

Some pastors and congregants kept the dialogue limited to matters of hygiene, but others voiced their anxieties over mingling germs with those labeled as social outcasts. "Physical and moral uncleanliness are unseparable," states an 1895 newspaper of the United Brethren. "The first steps on the ladder of moral purity are clean faces, clean bodies, clean clothes, clean food."[7]

The diversity of the church, they believed, constituted an inherent danger—"a rich opportunity for transmitting disease."[8] Looking to defend their fears theologically, some pastors argued that Communion is less about the relationship of an individual to the corporate body and more about the relationship between an individual and God.

Others feared that a focus on sanitation as the mode of purity in the church would turn worshipers away from the communion of believers and create class and racial divisions within the church.[9] "The Holy Communion is ordained to symbolize the union of the believer with Christ, and the union of all believers in One Body," argued one of the staunchest advocates for maintaining the common cup.[10]

Nevertheless, the individualized Communion practice took root in many Protestant churches. "It's more important that you do it than how you do it," said Jim Johnson, the pastor who designed the prepackaged portions of my first Communion, a century after the arguments about individual Communion began.[11]

Over the latter half of the twentieth century, evangelical churches continued to emphasize a shift in focus from corporate and corporal worship to that of an individual, spiritual experience of God. The content of sermons and songs, and their application to the Christian's life, took precedence over the rhythms and liturgies that once guided communities of faith. Biblical literacy took precedence over Church history, revealing a focus on individual salvation over and above communal worship.

At the same time, wariness about Christian practices that connect worshipers to their bodies grew. Movements like genuflections and signs of the cross were viewed by evangelical Protestants as rituals void of spiritual value. As these practices faded, they were replaced by anxieties about how to ensure the purity of the body, nutritionally and sexually.

The eighties and nineties saw a proliferation of books and sermons about Christian dieting as well as the rise of the sexual purity movement, both of which revealed an aspiration to use the body to honor God, alongside a fear of the body and its pleasure. These movements downplayed the body's physical needs and desires, and they minimized physical delight as a means of drawing into fellowship with God and with God's people. The goal was, as with the twentieth-century baking industry's relationship to yeast, to be free from "contamination." Or, put more simply, to maintain control.

I write this book a century after the introduction of industrialized bread altered the landscape of American baked goods, in the wake of another pandemic that has changed the ways we live and eat and worship. The waves of COVID-19 continue to ebb and flow, illuminating fears and fissures within churches, families, and neighborhoods. Questions proliferate about how to care for our own bodies and the bodies of our neighbors. What is our moral responsibility to limit the spread of disease? What impact does worshiping online have on our spiritual well-being? And how do we reckon with the necessities and harms of extended isolation?

Many adults who grew up in evangelical churches of the eighties and nineties find themselves in spiritual turmoil, grappling with the fruit of the disembodied theology of their upbringing. They are angered by the proliferation of spiritual and sexual abuse in the communities that raised them. They are grieving the absence of the fruitful marriages they were promised, if only they followed the purity rules. They are shocked over the blatant racism and sexism exhibited by the leaders who taught them to love as Jesus loved.

It was in this context, when the world's collective stress was at its peak, that men and women across the United States turned to bread for peace. The spring of 2020 saw grocery store shelves emptied of flour and yeast, while Google searches for bread recipes rose to all-time highs.[12] In seven months, King Arthur Baking Company sold twice as many five-pound bags of flour as they'd sold the entire previous year—not to mention the consumers who purchased fifty-pound bags when they couldn't find the smaller size.[13] The feel of dough brought grounding amid the loss of community and the loss of control.

God meets us in the baking and breaking of bread. In the same way, God communes with us through the broken but beautiful rhythms of the church—despite the church's bickering and division, despite the pain it inflicts. God is present with us in tangible ways in our hunger and our loneliness, our hurts and our longings—especially in the form of bread, broken and shared among God's people. In this sharing, we are taught to hunger all the more for the fullness of healing yet to come.

We continue to live in the tension of bread as blessing and bread as curse. While most of us don't experience the labor of growing and harvesting wheat, wheat allergies and the fear of carbohydrates abound. But bread still offers us a way forward, a way to heal our relationship to the body of Christ and to our own bodies—and to find delight in each. A robust understanding of bread makes plain to us the reasons that poor teaching on community and the body, born of Wonder Bread theology, failed to nourish a generation of Christians well.

As both a professional baker and a student of theology, I am grieved that decades of eaters (myself included) have feared bread and its ill effects on their bodies due to the reputation of industrialized loaves. Similarly, it grieves me that a generation of people who grew up in a Christian culture formed by the pursuit of sanitation and control dismiss their faith without knowledge of the tradition's rich capacity to meet them in their pain and fear.

Our relationship to theology and the church can be much like Wonder Bread: cheap, industrialized, lacking nourishment and flavor. We gravitate toward Wonder Bread not because we think it's the best, but because it's convenient and affordable. Sometimes we choose it because it tastes like home, and sometimes because we have no idea there's something better. But the life of Jesus and the story of Scripture, as well as the substance of bread itself, show us there is more.

"One does not live by bread alone," Jesus said to the tempter in the desert, "but by every word that comes forth from the mouth of God" (Matthew 4:4, NAB).

Jesus himself is both the Bread of life and the Word who was with God in the beginning. He is the Word that proceeds from the mouth of God, as well as the Bread we place in our own mouths. We can know

God on our tongues and in our bellies when hunger and loneliness and disappointment are too deep for words.

The beauty of this communion with God can't be adequately captured in theological terms. It resists being pinned down by words at all, though story, poetry, and recipe get us closer. The very point of God meeting us in this way is to remind us that the materiality of our lives and of God's world matters. The Bread of Life is not just a metaphor for spiritual truth: when we bake bread and break bread, both individually and in community, we know God in a rich, creative, and intimate way.

As soon as water hits flour, a series of transformations begins: amino acids uncoil, forming bonds to create a strong, sticky dough. The journey from flour to dough to bread depends on a succession of conversions—small deaths that make way for new life. The baker's task is not to follow a proper formula to ensure an exact end result but to read the environment, pull the ingredients together, and gently nudge the dough in the proper direction, all while trusting water and time to do most of the transforming.

In this way, bread mirrors the journey of faith.

Bread, like God, is not a mystery to be mastered or solved. It is at once simple—a mix of flour, water, yeast, and salt—and infinitely complex. Thousands of years after our ancestors made their first loaf, bakers are still learning new ways to pull flavor and texture from grain. We can commit our entire lives to the rhythms of baking, of drawing out the nuances of wheat, and still have more to learn. The goal should not be mastery in and of itself, but curiosity and joy. Breadmaking, like faith, is a craft to hone over the course of a lifetime, a truth that is at once exciting and liberating.

This book is about bread, and about *the* Bread, and about the muddled space between the two. It's the story of how God has met me in my baking and eating—as an insatiable child and a timid teen, as a world-traveling student and an underpaid pastry cook. It's the story of hunger and family, of friendship and unmet longing.

It's the story of a God who meets us in both sacred and mundane ways.

In the mixing and kneading, in the waiting and partaking, may God also meet you.

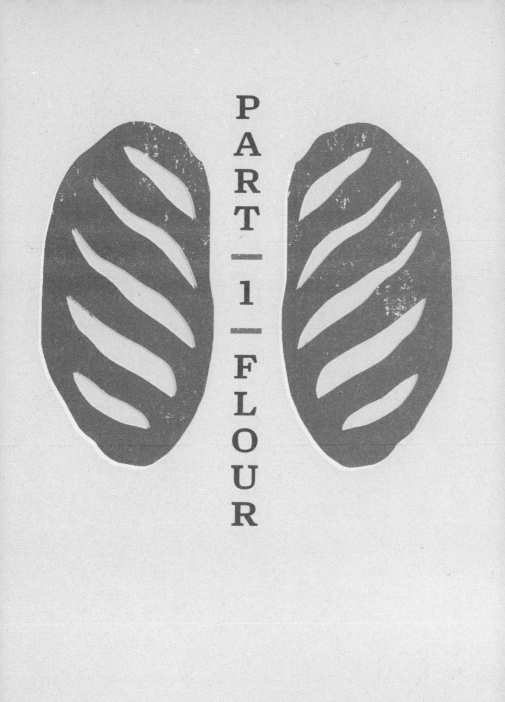

PART—1—FLOUR

Flour is the backbone of any loaf of bread.

Corn.

Rice.

Barley.

Wheat.

Each piece a creation of culture and agriculture:

the people who mix it,

the places that raise it,

the environment where it ferments and grows.

1

ON HUNGER

Give us this day our daily bread.

THE LORD'S PRAYER

RICHARDSON, TEXAS

Every day around the world, Christians mutter the Lord's Prayer.

Give us this day our daily bread.

Danos hoy el pan de este día.

Donne-nous aujourd'hui notre pain de ce jour.

When I was in high school, my French teacher opened each class with a group recitation of this prayer. While I'd read the words before, they weren't a regular part of my upbringing. In my church and in my family, the emphasis was on extemporaneous prayer, which was viewed as the most authentic form.

But something about this ritual ingrained the French words of the prayer into the rhythms of my body. Even now, as I sit curled in my red chair, sipping coffee and praying to start my day, I slip back into French for the final phrase: "For thine is the kingdom, the power, and the glory, *aux siècles des siècles.* Amen."

In this prayer, one simple substance functions as a metaphor for all our basic needs. In my own life, though, bread has served as far more than a symbol of God's presence. Actual bread, made of flour and water—and my own hunger for it—has been an ongoing reminder of the brokenness of my body, of relationships, and of this world, as well as Christ's presence in it all.

The way my hunger shapes me, the way it shapes my desires and my experience of the world, brings me both shame and joy.

In first grade, my class took a field trip to Great Harvest Bread Company. Clad in navy houndstooth jumpers and saddle oxfords, a dozen of us walked in a uniform line through the back of the bakery. We gaped at the fifty-pound bags of flour and the industrial mixers mushing all the ingredients together into a giant blob.

Hypnotized by the baker's movements, I felt as though I were watching a choreographed ballet: slice, weigh, shape; slice, weigh, shape; slice, weigh, shape. The baking crew laughed and chatted around the wooden workbench, their faces dusted with flour. As they filled trays and transferred them to racks alongside the oven, neither their hands nor their conversation slowed.

After the tour I described every detail of the bakery's operations to my mother—the bags of flour stacked taller than my three-and-a-half-foot frame, the mixing bowls deep enough to bathe in, the pile of dough that grew as the bakers divvied it up.

The next time Mom brought my older sister, Alyssa, and me to the bakery for a treat, I showed off what I'd learned. "That's the classic bread," I told her, pointing to the board of samples. "It's the base they use for everything. The nut-and-spice bread is made with the same dough. And that cheese one, too."

While Mom smeared our samples with the softened butter the store kept on hand, I babbled on about the bread. Our Great Harvest was small, with one children's table, one adult table, and only enough room for a short line, which meant that everyone behind us heard my recounting of the field trip too. Alyssa rolled her eyes at my incessant talking until at last it was time for us to pick out cinnamon rolls—each one as big as our face—to share with the family on Saturday morning.

As humans, we make the connection between hunger and communication in the first hours of life, wailing anytime we want to eat. We learn to make our hunger known long before we're capable of comprehending or articulating the need for our bellies to be full. As our caretakers feed us and cuddle us and nurture us, our affections for them are formed. In this way, our experience of the world is shaped through an interweaving of hunger and language and love, through our guttural longing for intimacy and food, out of which we eventually learn to speak.

While most children start communicating with words like *Mama* or *Dada*, announcing their affection for the ones who feed them, I was driven to speak by my sweet tooth. My first word, I am told, was *cookie*. It came out sounding a bit like "googie," but I was so adamant and so dynamic with my bodily gestures, toddling into the kitchen with hands and mouth open wide, that my parents understood. My second word, I am told, was *candy*.

As we gain independence, the link between our need for food and our need for companionship becomes less clear, apart from the vague recognition that the table can forge community. It's tempting to see food as nothing more than fuel, parceled out in calories and nutrient contents. In a world where prepackaged meals and drive-through lanes reign, where eating is something we fit in between work and exercise and caring for children, we often overlook the ways our daily hunger forms us.

Like language, though, the foods we eat, the ones we avoid, and the ones that connect us to family or to home shape our sense of who we are.

Soon after the fortieth-anniversary celebration at Richardson Heights, my family left the church in search of a smaller congregation— one where we could be known as more than the founding pastor's family. We were the first of the Vanderslices to defect from Baptist tradition, settling into a nondenominational Bible church a few miles away.

One morning, Pastor Charlie, the overall-wearing children's minister at North Highlands Bible, walked around the room handing out slips of bright green paper with a question on each one.

"Each Sunday I'll give you a question about the Bible," he told us, explaining the rules of his latest game. "The first person to leave a message on my answering machine with the right answer gets a prize: two McDollars."

My eyes bugged at the possibility of a McDonald's gift certificate. The one catch? We couldn't call before Monday.

As we drove home in our maroon minivan, I bombarded Mom with details from the backseat. "I'm going to call before I leave for school," I told her. "I bet no one else will call as early as 6:30!"

Alyssa and I spent the afternoon flipping through our Bibles, trying to find the name of the river where Naaman washed his leprosy away. We didn't have the Internet at our house yet, which meant we were on our own to find the answers.

The next morning before leaving for school, we dialed Pastor Charlie's office number and left a message: "Hi, Pastor Charlie," Alyssa opened. "This is Alyssa and Kendall Vanderslice, and we're calling with the answer to the Bible quiz."

"The River Jordan!" I shouted into the receiver when she passed the phone to me. "We found it in 2 Kings 5:14."

"We hope we're the first ones to call," Alyssa said in closing. Then we hung up and giggled, sure we'd won.

The next Sunday I skipped into Sunday school, passing over the box of donuts to find a seat near the front, where Pastor Charlie held the prized certificates.

"The winning call," he announced, "came in at 12:01 a.m."

My heart sank; our answer was more than six hours late. Pastor Charlie passed out a new set of question slips, peach colored this time. "What was Jesus' first temptation?" the paper read.

"Mom, we need to call at midnight!" Alyssa announced on the ride home. "We have to be the first."

We set our alarms for 11:57 so we could wake up and make the call. My alarm, however, did not go off.

At 2:15 I woke up in a panic and scrambled to the phone. "Hi, um, this is Kendall," I said in a groggy voice. "The answer is turning stones to bread."

Pastor Charlie soon amended the rules, no doubt thanks to the complaints of the parents of sleepless kids: no calls allowed before 7:00 on Monday morning. Instead of competing to win each Monday, those who called with the right answer every week could attend a dinner at the Magic Time Machine—a restaurant where servers dressed up like characters from TV shows and movies. With the promise of this meal in mind, I spent each Sunday afternoon scouring the Scriptures for trivia answers.

By May, my hours of study paid off. Only a handful of kids had earned the meal, and I was proud to be among them. One Monday evening, at the start of summer break, we piled into the church van. As Pastor Charlie drove us across town, the other kids chattered on about their favorite characters, wondering aloud who our server would be. I sat in silence, thinking about the menu. Mom had given me permission to order whatever I wanted.

At the time my family practiced a Christianized version of the hippie health movement. Much like the natural-food advocates in the 1970s, the "Hallelujah Diet" promised wellness and spiritual fulfillment to those who ate a diet of simple foods, who cared for their bodies and for the earth. Unlike the hippies, Hallelujah eaters attuned themselves to the nutritional wisdom hidden in the pages of Scripture—for instance, Adam and Eve's raw food habits in the Garden or Daniel's vegetarian restrictions in Nebuchadnezzar's kingdom. Meat and dairy were distinctly off limits. Bread was whole grain and preferably homemade, though the diet had little to say about the presence or absence of leaven. Our Great Harvest excursions (and my Magic Time Machine meal) were exceptions to the rules.

"Get back to the health you were created to have," the diet literature claimed, citing success at curing cancer and chronic pain. "When you get back to the Garden, you can live life fully, the way that God intended."

When Shaggy, the mystery-solving teen from the Scooby-Doo series, arrived at the table to take our orders, I asked for a cheeseburger, fries, and a Dr Pepper. I clapped with excitement when the food arrived, practically dancing in my seat. Juice from the patty dripped down my arms as I took the first bite, ketchup smearing my cheek.

———

When I was in elementary school, I often suffered from chronic stomachaches that sent me home early. My parents scraped by to provide us with a classical Christian education at a school that met in an Episcopal church (which, to my mother's elation, I pronounced Eh-PEE-scoh-pal) in the wealthy part of town.

Every morning we carpooled with two neighbors for the half-hour commute, driving from the small ranch-style neighborhoods of Richardson to the mansions of Highland Park. We'd arrive just in time to place our backpacks in the classroom and run a math drill before sauntering to the chapel to sing hymns. I excelled at the math drills, and I loved the hymns, but by the time we returned to the classroom afterward, my stomach cramps began.

"Can I please be excused to go to the bathroom?" I whispered to my teacher before sitting at my desk. I hid in the bathroom that connected our classroom to the one next door, blinking back tears.

"Are you okay in there, Kendall?" Mrs. Chester would ask when I was slow to emerge.

"I think I need to go home," I replied.

Skeptical of Western medicine, my mom took me to a series of naturopathic doctors who attempted to diagnose my digestion woes. After losing her biological mother to lung cancer at the age of five, Mom was fastidious about both health and prayer. She, too, experienced on-going stomach troubles, and she sought to keep the pain away with a mix of supplements and dietary alterations.

"Give her digestive enzymes," one practitioner recommended after examining my blood work, which revealed nothing. "That should do the trick."

We shopped at Whole Foods back when it was a quirky Texas health chain, and we were the only patrons free from tattoos, piercings, and artificial hair colors. Every morning I washed a five-pound bag of carrots for Mom to juice and chugged powdered barley mixed with cranberry juice and flaxseed oil. In music class, our teacher would start the day with a game that involved singing out what we ate for breakfast. While my classmates identified Pop-Tarts and bagels and English muffins as their morning fuel, I had to tell them, every day, about my vegetable juice.

"That smells nasty," a boy in my class said one day as I choked down a salad smothered in green goddess dressing. My cheeks burned as I held my own nose, trying to mask the flavor of alfalfa sprouts and raw squash. I looked over at his Wonder Bread peanut butter and jelly, imagining how it must taste. Sometimes Mom would pack me a sandwich, too—cashew butter, honey, and a handful of shredded carrots tucked between two slices of homemade bread—but most often I went to school with a salad. I closed the container and placed it back inside my lunch box before running off to play four square with a friend.

"I'm hungry," I told my mom on the way from school to church choir practice. "Can I have a slice of pizza after choir?"

"What happened to your lunch?" she asked.

"I didn't eat it," I whispered.

"Then you need to eat it now," she replied.

I opened the container to find the lettuce wilted from the weight of the dressing and the warmth of my bag. I gagged as I choked it down.

By the time I was in third grade, my family's dietary habits had come in handy. The school had switched campuses, now meeting at Congregation Shearith Israel, a conservative synagogue five miles from the Episcopal church. While students weren't required to keep kosher at lunch, we did have strict limitations on the foods we could bring. Among the most important rules: no pork, and no mixing of meat and dairy. The Vanderslice children were well practiced in this regard. Though I hated telling my classmates about my vegetable juice and flaxseed oil, our diet meant I never once brought a lunch that broke the rules. This, at least, brought my mind a bit of ease.

During Passover, the synagogue provided food for us, ensuring that we didn't bring wheat or legumes into the building. We'd carry our plates along a buffet of platters, served by smiling women wearing lace kippahs. Their dietary rhythms told the story of God's presence throughout history, year after year. It connected them to generations of Jews who remembered God's deliverance through both their abstinence and their feasts. Their eating habits were an act of submission to God, who in turn offered identity and belonging through these shared meals.

Hallelujah eaters, on the other hand, had about as many rules but none of the traditions. We considered this to be a good thing. Our diet wasn't mandated by religion; rather, we chose it out of a desire to care for our bodies, and we believed God had given us the blueprint for how to care for them well. Our eating got straight to the point: to rid ourselves of the pain endemic to being human in a fallen world. We would eat our way to wellness—to God's best for us. We would prove our faithfulness not through communal identity but through the quest for health.

Eating has the power to forge community and shape our identity.

At best food fosters a sense of belonging among those who eat in similar ways, a reminder that our longing for community and our need for food go hand in hand. For most of history, eating has been tied to cultural or religious identity, but even without those underpinnings, we manage to create our own new dietary identities. Paleo. Keto. Vegan. The list goes on.

At worst, though, food can mark a form of social isolation. Whether the family diet sparks criticism from classmates or allergies prevent us from sharing a meal with others, food is also a reminder that God's good creation has been marred.

The temptation to pine for Eden is about as strong as the temptation whispered to Eve by the snake. We look back and long for a time before hunger, before pain, before eating became the site of our cosmic undoing. We wonder how we can approximate a blissful existence here and now, creating our own lists of forbidden foods and trying to enforce extreme levels of self-control.

But the story of Scripture is not one of returning to a life before the Fall. To pine for Eden is to overlook the ways God is at work in the world now. Scripture tells a story of God's ongoing redemption and God's promise of what's to come: a renewed creation, where the scars of our present brokenness are crafted into something new—something more beautiful than the Garden where it all began. A city where the tree of life yields its fruit all year round,[1] where there will be no more death and no more mourning, no crying and no more pain.

For now, though, we live in between these two realities, where our bodies ache and hunger, where we feel shame and regret. We can't avoid the world we live in, where the emergence of new life, whether out of the womb or out of the soil, demands our sweat and tears. It's a reality where parents pass down their allergies and their anxieties, along with their unique methods of cooking and feeding and showing they care. The history of humanity is a history of learning how to contend with our need for food and for love in the reality of this present brokenness.

"Everyone gets to choose one book," Gramma said, pulling her gold sedan into a parking spot in front of Sam's Club. "And stay with me while we walk through the samples."

"What kind of cake will we get?" I asked from the backseat.

"Whatever kind you want," she replied. "Just make sure Alyssa stays away!"

School breaks spent with my mom's parents in Houston were our dietary jubilee. We baked cakes from box mixes for Gramma's Bible study meetings, and we made broccoli corn bread to accompany Dedaddy's favorite vegetable beef soup.

On one visit, Alyssa assured us she knew how to operate the oven, preheating it while we mixed the batter. We came to check on the finished product forty-five minutes later, only to find it burned on top and raw in the middle.

"Oh, Alyssa!" Gramma hollered. "You broiled the thing!"

Though we had harbored a mix of disappointment and anger on the day of the baking flop, with time the memory became a joke. I was now the designated baker, making treats for the women of First Baptist Humble. While the cake was fun to make and serve, the true taste of the promised land came in the scoops of Blue Bell ice cream we would heap on top—a ritual we undertook every night before bed.

Upon our return home from Houston, Mom would roll her eyes at the new fullness in our cheeks. She'd tell us about her visits to her own grandparents when she and her sister were girls—waking up to the sound of bacon sizzling on the other side of the trailer, watching Mamaw roll out biscuits every morning. She'd tell us how Gramma called them butterballs when they arrived back home.

At the end of each break, when it came time to go back to school, my stomachaches returned.

I was anxious about the timed math drills and the weekly vocabulary tests, not to mention the social interactions in class and on the playground. I couldn't handle the stress of striving for both perfection and belonging.

"You always ace the practice tests," a kid in our carpool whined one day when I told my mom about my grade. Every week I was nervous before the test began and then embarrassed over my excitement when I did well. "It isn't fair," my carpool friend added.

Another day I got in trouble because a seatmate was talking to me. As punishment, he and I had to sit out during the first half of recess.

"Do you understand why you're sitting out today?" the recess monitor asked me when my time-out was up.

I wept as I recounted the story to her. "He kept talking to me, even though I tried to tell him to stop! Then we both got into trouble, but I didn't do anything!"

I begged my parents to homeschool me like my friends at dance and at church. The summer before fourth grade, they relented.

Determined to offer me an education equivalent to what I was leaving behind, Mom pored over textbooks and creative-writing curriculum. Most important, she arranged field trips for my other homeschooled friends and me. After our Great Harvest excursion, we toured the back of Mrs Baird's, the famous Texas bread manufactory.

At Mrs Baird's, there were no fifty-pound bags of flour or laughter around the baker's bench. Instead, the grain was contained in giant drums, and the dough was divvied up along a conveyor belt. Still, my eyes gaped at the rows of deck ovens while the scent of melted butter and caramelized starches enveloped me.

Although we never purchased Mrs Baird's offerings at the grocery store, there was no doubt about her iconic status in Texas history. Launching her business just before the start of the Great Depression—when industrial bakers recommended that women leave the professional bread to men—Ninnie Baird delivered loaves around town on foot, then by bike and by carriage, and eventually by fleets of trucks. After her death in 1961, the Texas State Senate declared her "a living example for mothers, wives, business executives, Christians, and good people the world over."[2] In the decades since, bags of her buns have graced fellow-ship hall tables at churches across the state. From feeding rambunctious children at Sunday potlucks to satiating mourners at funerals, her bread is present in every phase of the Texas churchgoer's communal life.

At the factory, there were no bakers slicing or shaping the grow-ing dough by hand. While the movements between each human and machine still followed a distinct choreography, the joviality was missing. The manufactory didn't grip me the same way Great Harvest had, but the trip still lodged itself in my memory. Mrs Baird's buns weren't the weekend cinnamon rolls or the special-occasion treats; they were the ever-present blue bag. Nutritionally lacking, perhaps, but constant. And, as such, a comfort, too.

2

ON BELONGING

This is my Body, which is given for you.

THE BOOK OF COMMON PRAYER,
"THE HOLY EUCHARIST"

DALLAS, TEXAS

In the thirteenth century, medieval theologian Thomas Aquinas wrote a collection of arguments about how to serve Holy Communion. In it, he argues for wheat bread as the only appropriate representation of the Body of Christ. While dense barley breads were common among the poor at the time of Christ, Aquinas assumed that Jesus himself would have served bread made from higher quality wheat.[1]

A kernel of wheat contains three parts: the bran, the germ, and the endosperm. Whole wheat flour preserves all three parts of the grain, while white flour is made by sifting away the bran and the germ that weigh down a loaf. In recent years, whole grains have grown in popularity among bakers and consumers, thanks to the flavor and nutrient density they lend to bread. But this preference for whole-grain baking is new: for most of history, white flour has been considered the wheat of the elite. Given the laborious process of growing, harvesting, threshing, and grinding wheat, only those with means could afford to make their bread out of such a small portion of the grain.

In Aquinas's time, bread made of the finest white wheat was the only bread deemed suitable for the sacrament, out of respect for Christ's Body. Today, though, bakers pride themselves in the ability to craft loaves made with the entire grain—a skill that requires long fermentation to soften the fibrous parts.

"My mother was a complex woman," Mom opened, her voice shaking as she gripped the script she'd written. Her words drew nods and tearful chuckles as she recounted the Gramma Ruth we'd known over the last twenty years—the one who led Bible studies and stocked the deep freeze with ice cream anytime it went on sale. The funeral-home pews were split between extended family and church family, though not a single blood relative of Gramma Ruth's was there.

"Ruth was a witness to the transforming love of God," Mom continued.

Mom skirted the details of Gramma's early years of motherhood. She married my grandfather just a year after his first wife (also named Ruth) passed away. Gramma had just turned thirty, a middle-school English teacher, proud to have earned a master's degree in education.

Like my own parents, she and Dedaddy met at church. My grandfather, still grieving, ached for a partner and someone to help raise his girls. In just a matter of months, Gramma stepped into life as a wife and a mother of four—two sons who were barely a decade her junior and daughters ages six and four.

With her hand trembling against the mic stand, my mother told of the night before the birth of her own fourth child. She'd sat with Gramma on the bed, Gramma's hand on Mom's belly, feeling for hiccups or kicks.

"You talk about God like you know him," Gramma said. "Like he's an old friend."

Mom placed her hand alongside Ruth's to feel the baby's movement, considering the ways she'd clung to God's love during the years when Ruth's tenderness was absent.

"I just don't see him that way," Ruth continued.

Her softening had begun before this point, like the fibrous pieces of wheat in their first fermentation. Gramma had never been able to birth children of her own. Whether her bitterness was caused by late marriage and infertility or her fear of comparison to her husband's late wife, she scarred the family with her sharp language and cruel tone. While the older grandchildren remember her harsher days, the younger ones experienced her softening. But that night, when she asked her swollen-bellied stepdaughter to pray for her, something deeper shifted.

"She was never the same after that," Mom said to close her eulogy before sliding back into the pew between her sister and me.

An hour later, our family filled the fellowship hall at First Baptist Humble, which smelled of crispy fried onions and cream of chicken soup, the scents of Southern Baptist hospitality. Mom admired the buffet before poking her head into the kitchen to thank the women washing dishes.

"I wonder how many meals she prepared like this," Mom mused as she sat down beside me. I picked at my roll, still laced with the flavor of its blue plastic bag. I kept thinking of the story Mom had told, of that night twenty years before.

I'd never heard it before.

I was ten years old the night my mom and grandmother prayed. We'd just moved from Richardson to Lake Highlands—just down the road from the Bible church. After years of prayer, God (and my dad) agreed to Mom's pleas for a second son. Or so she assumed. The baby's gender hadn't been confirmed by ultrasound, only maternal instinct and a few sly comments from the obstetrician.

Homeschooling seemed to appease the anxiety that upset my stomach, allowing me to structure my school day around my own best rhythms. By my choice, I woke up each morning around five o'clock to tick off tasks in my planner:

1. Complete a math worksheet (or sometimes two).
2. Read a chapter in a history textbook.
3. Write a summary of the history reading.
4. Read a chapter in a work of classic literature.
5. Write a summary of that reading too.
6. Learn new vocabulary words.

Then I'd wash carrots for juicing and go back to bed for a nap while my sister groaned and got ready for school. At lunchtime, Mom allowed me to sit with her and watch an episode of *A Baby Story*, a show she hoped would prepare me for our own family's upcoming change. Each episode followed a family through the latter half of pregnancy all the way to the birth, filming their nursery preparations, doctor appointments, and hopes and dreams for the child.

I rested my hand on Mom's belly, feeling for hiccups or kicks.

"When the parents said they 'started trying,'" I asked, "did that mean they'd begun to pray for a baby like we did?"

Mom stifled a laugh.

"Mm, yeah, something like that," she responded before suggesting we move on to our ancient history lesson and a discussion about the ways it overlapped with stories in the Bible.

Mom was scheduled for an induction on the morning of March 1, 2001. Alyssa had been born two weeks late and too broad shouldered to fit through the birth canal, so the rest of us were induced ten days early.

The night before the baby was due to arrive—while Mom was sitting with Gramma on her bed—I asked for prayers in our AWANA circle. The Wednesday-night AWANA program was a staple in evangelical churches at the time, its name standing for "Approved Workmen Are

Not Ashamed." Through games, songs, and memorization incentives, we were trained to be proud of and knowledgeable about our faith tradition. After reciting long passages of Scripture, students received jewels to place in a plastic crown before one of the leaders closed the night with prayer.

"We go to the hospital at seven o'clock, which is when they'll give her the Pitocin," I explained. "We expect she'll get an epidural soon after that, but it depends on how her labor progresses."

A couple of girls in the circle snickered, and I felt my cheeks begin to color. Our leader thanked me for sharing my concern, holding back a smile of her own. I wasn't sure what I'd done, but I sensed in their giggles that I'd said something wrong. I couldn't hide the evidence of shame building on my face, but I sealed my lips to avoid any more mistakes.

Unlike most crops, which are planted in the spring, wheat for bread making (often called winter wheat) is planted in the fall. When wheat is planted shortly before a frost, it stores up energy by sprouting and burrowing its roots down into the soil. As temperatures drop for the winter, the plants release a substance that protects the cell membranes, preventing them from freezing so the roots can continue to grow.

Wheat doesn't have to be planted this way—the grain can be sown in the spring, after the soil has softened and warmed. But spring wheat lacks the endurance necessary to make good bread. When the plant undergoes a winter hardening, made possible by the sprouts that take root in the fall, the protein in the grain develops properties that enable it to withstand long fermentations, providing flavor and structure to a loaf.

If that evening was the launch of Gramma's softening, for me it was the start of a hardening off. Like the toughening of wheat as the ground freezes, the shift wasn't sudden; it was more of a growing realization that I didn't quite belong.

My parents hadn't yet settled on a name, but the options—Lars or Boston—were sure to consign my brother to a life of ridicule. They'd agreed to a girl's moniker early on, just in case: Emma Claire. Emma in honor of Gramma's full name (Emma Ruth), and Claire in honor of the Southern love for double names.

Having accompanied Mom to every doctor's appointment and feeling well versed in delivery-room expectations after months of *A Baby Story* episodes, I asked permission to observe the birth. The nurses scoffed at the idea of a ten-year-old watching her mother writhing in pain, but when I proved inconsolable, they agreed. Alyssa, at twelve years old, was stationed with me on our mother's left; our dad was on her right. As the baby's head emerged, the nurses allowed us to sneak around for a closer look. I was mesmerized by the miracle of birth, solidifying my plans to have ten children of my own. Alyssa, on the other hand, was horrified.*

As the baby slid out the rest of the way, the doctor declared, "It's a girl!"

"No, it's not," Mom responded, delusional from hormones and pain.

"It is," the doctor replied with a chuckle.

"Emma Claire," Dad whispered, grinning as he snipped the umbilical cord.

In the months that followed, I rocked Emma Claire at every opportunity. I clothed her in frilly dresses and pushed the stroller when we went into stores.

I wonder if people will think I'm her mother, I pondered as we strolled around, giddy at the thought that I could look so mature.

I stretched headbands with giant flowers around Emma Claire's skull and snapped photos of us in matching hats. Mom said we could blow up the photos and frame them for the bedroom the baby and I would soon share. When we picked up the developed images from the pharmacy, I noticed the rolls of my own belly, accentuated by the horizontal stripes of my top that crept up where Emma Claire kicked her legs. In one particular image, she and I shared a double chin.

---

* Twenty years later, I have neither witnessed nor participated in any other births. Alyssa went on to become a labor and delivery nurse and, at the time of this writing, has given birth to one child. Neither of us were irreparably scarred by this event.

"I don't need these on the wall," I said, tucking the pictures back in their envelope. *It's a weird angle*, I told myself.

On Sunday afternoons, I embarked on the quarter-mile trek up Church Road to visit my best friend, Rebecca. As soon as I arrived at her house, I would raid her pantry and put together a snack. Rebecca and I held a weekly tradition of making "concoctions," using whatever ingredients called to us from the pantry.

Typically these concoctions involved a mixture of candies, perhaps boxed brownie mix or cake mix, sometimes ice cream and sprinkles. Nothing on my own kitchen shelves enticed me like the bags and boxes that lined her cupboards—not the fresh dates or the lentils, not the sprouts mom incubated on the kitchen counter, not even the homemade almond milk that we mixed with maple syrup and a touch of cinnamon.

"Do you eat this much at home?" Rebecca's mom once asked as I scoured her cabinet for ingredients.

My stomach dropped. I offered a stifled chuckle in return, attempting to smile but incapable of hiding my reddening cheeks. I turned back toward the cabinet to mask my face as best I could, even though I no longer remembered what I was looking for.

When Rebecca's mom offered pizza rolls or leftover pigs in a blanket, I never refused. I took full advantage of each opportunity to feast on the treats I didn't have access to at home. In those brief moments of gustatory pleasure, I imagined what it was like to be normal, to shop where other kids shopped and eat what other kids ate. But these attempts to find belonging through food left me feeling perpetually out of place. Despite our nutrient-packed pantry, I was not thin like my friends.

My friends and I were at the age when girls started talking about numbers on the scale. I'd surpassed the ninety-pound mark while they were still in the seventies; I knew this because Rebecca and our friend KK casually mentioned their weight while jumping cannonballs into the deep end of the pool. I never said my own number aloud, but I checked it every day, sneaking into my mother's bathroom and pulling out her green scale.

Rebecca and KK exchanged swimsuits and wore each other's shorts. When we sat together in the backseat of Rebecca's Suburban, I noticed how their legs remained the same width from the knee up while mine widened considerably mid-thigh. I held my hand over the flab to envision how I might look if I chopped off the unwanted parts, calculating ways to curb my hunger and ride my bike more.

While I'd been taught to protect myself against shame over my faith, I had no shield against the shame I felt about my body. Neither my love for God nor my memorization of Scripture—not even my biblical diet—could conceal the fact that my body was not like that of my friends.

———

At ballet, KK hung out with the popular girls. While I tripped over my feet whenever I learned a new jump or turn, they all seemed confident and at ease. Somehow their bodies knew what to do at the barre. They always looked cool, keeping up with new trends in leotards and tights. They chatted in the dressing room until class began, twisting their hair into elaborate buns.

Too shy to join them, I waited in a chair just outside the classroom. For weeks, I saved my money to buy a black ballet bag like the ones the popular girls used, the kind with *Capezio* stitched along the top.

"I like your bag!" one of them commented after class the first day I brought it in.

My cheeks burned and my voice cracked as I said thanks. I couldn't believe she'd noticed.

"You know you can hang out with us in the dressing room," KK told me one afternoon when we met at her house to play.

I was awed by KK's self-confidence and natural humor, with both adults and peers. Whenever she joined my family for dinner, she kept all of us laughing, unafraid to say whatever came to mind. I felt protected under the shadow of her friendship.

"We're walking to the Chinese restaurant down the street," KK told me one day during a break between class and rehearsal. "Want to join?"

I'd packed my lunch, and I didn't have money to buy extra food, but I agreed to tag along.

I was thrilled at the chance to join the girls on their excursion—and terrified that I would say something weird that would keep me from getting invited again. So I walked just behind them, silent the entire way.

"Is everything okay?" KK asked when we got back to class.

"Yeah," I responded with a grin. "Why?"

"Oh, uh, nothing," she replied.

The next summer KK and I spent two weeks at Ballet Magnificat!, a Christian ballet intensive in Jackson, Mississippi. The program sought to train professional ballerinas with a healthier relationship to their bodies than was common in the classical ballet world. KK's sister had attended the program years before, so she came along to move us into the dorm.

"Make sure you wipe down the mattress before you put your sheets on," she warned us as we drove across Louisiana. "You never know who has been sleeping there."

"Don't worry—I brought the disinfectant!" their mom chimed in from the front.

"They won't let you call home the first week because they don't want you to get too homesick," her sister interjected. "You can call the second week, though."

"The ice cream in the cafeteria is delicious," KK added. "You can eat it every meal if you want."

The first morning, KK and I walked together to the cafeteria for breakfast. I prepared a full bagel dressed in shmear—a white bagel, which never would have passed at home. We sat down with two other girls from our floor. They split half of a wheat bagel between them. The next morning I followed suit, asking KK if she wanted to share. By the end of the two weeks, I'd shifted to eating only a quarter of a bagel a day, skipping the ice cream that everyone claimed was so good.

I enjoyed the light-headed feeling that arrived midway through our barre routine. The sensation of hunger connected me to my body in a new way; it showed me my ability to exert control. We took three to four classes a day, and in each one, instructors taught us to focus on our core. The strength of my stomach was more apparent to me through its emptiness; I felt the way the center of my body drove the movements of my arms and legs.

"Inhabit the music," the instructor said. "Feel the ways your neck, your fingers, and your elbows should respond."

I didn't quite understand what she meant, but I liked the idea. Rather than thinking my way into the movements, I needed to *feel* my way into them.

In the afternoons we took classes on improvisational dance, learning to use dance as a form of prayer. Unlike our other classes, we weren't given any choreography to follow. Instead, each exercise was a chance to practice moving our bodies in response to the music. But the freedom to move in any way I pleased sparked the same sense of dis-belonging I felt among my peers. My body didn't know what to do. It was the structure of ballet, not the freedom of improv, that provided enough safety for me to worship through the movements of my neck, my knees, my hands.

In chapel every morning, we listened to the testimonies of company members who had wrecked their bodies attempting to achieve the wisp-thin ballerina look and who had been healed by God, freed from their disordered relationship to eating.

Sitting in that sanctuary seat with my belly growling, I listened to their stories of liberation—and I looked forward to the possibility of trading swimsuits with KK and Rebecca one day soon.

3

ON CONTROL

Almighty God, to you all hearts are open, all desires known.

THE BOOK OF COMMON PRAYER,
"THE HOLY EUCHARIST"

In the late Middle Ages, the renunciation of food was considered one of the greatest expressions of ascetic devotion to God. Extreme fasting was born not out of a dualistic revulsion of the flesh—a belief that the body is inferior to the soul. Rather, it was born out of a desire to plumb the beauty of the Incarnation, the doctrine that Christ's humanity saves us, both body and soul.

By renouncing ordinary food and drink, religious men and women opened themselves to deeper communion with God through the mystical union of the Eucharist. In consuming Christ's Body, they assimilated God's Body into their own. "Eating God in the host . . . focused and transcended all hunger," writes historian Caroline Walker Bynum.[1] In addition to the self-sacrifice involved in renouncing food, the asceticism also included serving others, as those who fasted donated the food they would have otherwise eaten to the poor.

This form of religious asceticism was particularly compelling to women of the era. Food, and the preparation of it, was one of the few resources women could exert control over. In a world where renunciation was a form of worship, abstaining from food was at once an act of devotion and a reclamation of agency.

Though the devotion of these saints is worthy of admiration, it's important to note the physical and emotional repercussions of such renunciation. Their fasting was not performed to shape the body into a particular cultural ideal, but the result mirrored disordered eating today. The pursuit of full-bodied communion with God wove itself together with a pursuit of control, such that the two became difficult to differentiate.

Half a millennium later, this comingling desire for communion and control continues to weave its way into our relationships to food.

—————

The summer after my freshman year of high school, I spent seven weeks living in downtown Chicago—at Wabash and 11th Street, in the old Roosevelt University dorms. Each morning I'd make the two-block trek down Wabash to the Ballet Chicago studios with a group of fellow dancers, our hair clipped back in French twists, mesh bags of pointe shoes knocking at our sides.

Ballet Chicago's summer intensive was an audition-only program for dancers who had been denied summer training spots in New York and Seattle. Those in attendance were slightly above-average ballerinas training at top-tier schools, each of us determined to prove we could rise to the same level as our peers back home.

At 9:00 every morning, our instructor Patricia led us through a barre routine, her bracelets clacking and chiffon shirts swaying as she demonstrated each *port de bras*. We kept the windows of the seventh-floor studio open to the humid Chicago air, the hollow thump of stiff pointe shoes on Marley flooring overpowering the honks and sirens of the street below. Our accompanist lost herself in every piece of music, fingers and forearms flying over the keys. On many occasions Patricia would interrupt the pianist's reverie with a firm clap to let her know we'd finished the combination.

I watched my arms in the mirror, adjusting them centimeter by centimeter until my muscles remembered the lines they were supposed to form. Structure, muscle control, elongated limbs—these are the features that garner attention from instructors and artistic directors, especially in girls who still have a few more years left to train. Control, I had. Elongated muscles, I was working on. But I could not help the length of my limbs. At five foot two, my legs weren't growing anymore. My remaining years for training were closing in, and I struggled to get the attention of instructors.

In the afternoons we took modern dance, Pilates, ballet partnering, and character class. A few evenings a week, I'd return to the studio to take adult drop-in classes, an antidote to the inevitable late-night snacking I'd do if I watched a movie in my dorm room.

Two summers before, my family had relocated once again—this time to the Midwest, for my dad's job. The only faction of Vanderslices to defect from Baptist tradition soon became the only faction to defect from Texas as well. Aside from a maternal uncle and some cousins I'd hardly met, we didn't know anyone in Saint Louis. About the same time we learned we'd be moving three states away, we also learned that Mom was pregnant with baby number five. Though I loved babies and was interested in the idea of another brother (they confirmed it was a boy this time), I was not interested in the instability of more life change. A pubescent body plus a move were more than enough transition for me. I cried myself to sleep each night at the thought of leaving Rebecca and KK, and of the daunting task of navigating new friendships.

When I wasn't crying (and sometimes even when I was), I spent my final months in Texas researching ballet schools. The options were more limited than they'd been in Dallas, and once I ruled out the Russian-style studios (I had been trained in Balanchine, a different form), there were only two to choose from: the school attached to the city's professional ballet company (twelve miles from our new home) and a studio owned by Christians that incorporated theater and art into their repertoire (three miles from our new home).

One day shortly before we moved, I lamented to KK that nothing seemed like as good a fit as Dallas Ballet Center—I didn't trust the technique taught at the Christian studio, and my mom didn't want to drive me twelve miles to ballet every day.

"Why don't you quit?" she asked.

The thought hadn't occurred to me. I could pick up another hobby or try my hand at another sport. I hadn't exhibited any kind of exceptional talent in dance that would have proven wasteful to throw away, and my legs weren't growing any longer.

"But I don't want to," I replied.

Her question prompted me to prove my commitment to the art: not only did I want to keep dancing, I *needed* to. I needed to give it every ounce of my time, my energy, my body. I needed somewhere to channel my newfound understanding of the precariousness of life, of the changing nature of bodies and homes and friends. So on the heels of my family's cross-country move, I devoted myself to the craft. Sensing my drive, or at least my depression, my parents agreed to the long commute to dance school.

For two years, I stuffed my days with classes and rehearsals. I weighed myself on Mom's green scale each morning, and sometimes in the afternoons and evenings as well. I examined my body in the mirror, especially concerned with the way my belly protruded beyond my budding breasts and with the thickness of my quads and calf muscles (signs I was not relying on my inner thighs at the barre). I read dance magazines and created spreadsheets for various auditions—the high-caliber programs plus one or two safety schools, Ballet Chicago among them.

I set the alarm for 5:30 every morning and worked out on Dad's elliptical machine. I did homework while sitting in the splits, and I kept a log of every calorie, along with every gram of fat, protein, and sugar. I researched how many calories various activities burned and calculated the time it should take me to lose the necessary weight. For all my aspirations, I didn't have a goal weight in mind—I just wanted to be thin enough for someone to tell me I'd make it in the ballet world.

With all this work, I gained a bit of respect from the teachers at Saint Louis Ballet School. By the end of my summer at Ballet Chicago, I hoped to earn a place in the pre-professional level along with my peers. Day after day, I watched the definition form between my shoulder blades. A week before the program's end, I had a meeting with Patricia and her husband, co-owners of Ballet Chicago, to discuss my future.

"You're a good little dancer," Patricia's husband said, leaning against Patricia's desk.

Patricia, seated across from me, pursed her lips. My weight was the unspoken concern hovering in the room.

"Don't eat anything white," she told me. "No potatoes. No pasta. Definitely no bread."

I returned to Saint Louis that fall with permission to register for the highest level of ballet classes. To maintain momentum, I doubled up my class load, arriving early to dance with the level below. As a sophomore in high school, I itched to spend Friday evenings with my peers. Occasionally I joined a group of friends after rehearsal, bringing a salad to our movie nights so as not to be tempted by the pizza.

At the recommendation of my artistic director, Gen, I hired a nutritionist. He prescribed a protein powder that contained all the necessary nutrients, and he mapped out my daily meals:

8:00   shake
10:30   banana
12:00   another shake, this time with salad
3:00   one slice of Ezekiel 4:9 sprouted bread (the kind that
        must remain frozen to prevent mold)
6:00   one last shake and a vegetable stir-fry (no oil)

I'd wake up at 5:30 the next morning for a workout on the elliptical before beginning the meal routine over again. Every day was the same rhythm, and the pounds slid away. I envisioned the movie of my life with each stroke of the elliptical. The short, stubby ballerina who beat the odds, proving her worth to doubting teachers and wowing audiences worldwide. I could see the *Rocky* montage already, but with frozen prophetic bread instead of eggs.

Gen assured my parents I was too smart to give in to the temptation of disordered eating. The professional girls subsisted off coffee and cigarettes, the former to give them energy and the latter to suppress hunger. But if I kept to the plan I would be fine, he promised. We all wanted to believe it was true, so we ignored the evidence to the contrary, even as my nails broke and my hair thinned, and as my obsession with food took over my every waking thought.

When *Nutcracker* auditions rolled around once again, I was cast as an understudy to my peers. As disappointed as I was, I attended every rehearsal, learning all ten spots in "Waltz of the Flowers" should anyone get sick or injured.

"You look as skinny as everyone else onstage," my sister whispered at the end of our sixteenth show.

It's an odd tension: the human need to find mooring without getting stuck. To belong without losing track of who you are. To become strong enough to withstand the fluctuations of the seasons without turning so stiff that you wound the people you love.

In Christian tradition, we say that humans are created in the image of a triune God—a God who is in perpetual communion with creation, as well as with all three persons of the Trinity: Father, Son, and Holy Spirit. Humans are created with a need for communion as well—communion with God and with one another, communion with our bodies and with the created world. We are created to know God and to navigate the world through our bodies, not just with our minds.

We sense this need for the integration of body, mind, and soul—for tactile expressions of relationship—even if we don't fully understand it. And we fumble in our attempts to satisfy this inexplicable longing. Sometimes we lean so far into the desire to connect with our bodies that we fail to consider the impact of our pleasure or pain on ourselves or on those around us. Whether through sex, or the withholding of it, or through food, or the restriction of it, we can abuse the gifts intended to draw us into relationship with God and with others.

Other times we focus so intently on the desire to connect with God in our minds that we overlook the ways God's creation is designed to guide us into God's love. We ignore the fact that both physical need and physical pleasure can deepen our intimacy with the one who created us.

These misguided attempts to connect with our body or mind don't end up meeting our longing; instead, they amplify it. The pursuit of communion turns into a pursuit of control, and in time the pursuit itself controls us.

Sometimes, though, within our fumbling, we strike the proper chord. We taste an orange so sweet we can't help but marvel at the God who made it grow. Or we face a defeat so devastating we can't help but offer God back the reins. We carry these glimpses of God's provision with us as we move forward through our next round of fumbling until we find our footing again. With practice and attention, we can learn the art of such communion. As with kneading dough, we learn to sense when to work and when to let go, trusting that God meets us just beyond the grasp of our control.

Given my own propensity for anxiety, this practice involves fumbling more often than not. But slowly God is teaching me how to loosen my grip, holding me when I'm too worn down to hold on anymore.

In January, Saint Louis Ballet announced plans to perform George Balanchine's famous *Serenade*. I'd begun learning the ballet over the summer in Chicago. The piece opens with seventeen women lined up diagonally on stage, right arms raised, hands flexed. Still. The music begins with force and then crashes before repeating itself in a more tender tone. Every dancer moves in unison, making a simple plucking motion and then allowing her wrist to fall to her temple.

I cried the first time our reverential pianist played the song; six months later it hadn't yet lost its hold on me. As I raised my arm, wrist falling to my temple, I felt the melody move me more than any worship song at church or at school.

To perform a Balanchine number, a company must receive permission from the Balanchine Trust and learn the choreography from one of its approved instructors to ensure the purity of the famed choreographer's vision. We were appointed Patricia from Ballet Chicago, her bracelets clanking and her chiffon tops flowing. She would be with us for a week to teach us the piece.

Most of my peers were homeschooled so they could focus on their training, but by this point, I'd gone back to private school. I took the week off for rehearsal, arranging for my notes to be sent home with Alyssa. During our lunch breaks, I would catch up on my reading.

The Friday before Patricia's arrival, Gen pulled me aside.

"You don't need to come next week," he told me, "if you don't want to."

I wanted to.

"You won't be cast, so you probably shouldn't skip school."

My friends at school knew about my planned week off. The teachers did too. Everyone was aware of my strict dietary plan and my determination to dance professionally. I couldn't stand the embarrassment of going to school that week, of letting people know I'd failed to secure the desired role. So I attended rehearsals anyway. I stood in the back corner of the studio morning and afternoon for six days straight, trying to take up as little space as possible.

Over the next two months I attended daily rehearsals, followed by tech and dress rehearsals once we moved into the theater. I warmed up before every show and stood in the wings, just in case enough dancers and understudies got injured that they would need to place me—the fourth understudy—in a role.

But everyone danced through their injuries, and I convinced myself it was a valuable experience nonetheless. Soon after, I attended auditions for summer intensives.

I didn't get in.

Still, I took two technique classes every Saturday, one on flat and one on pointe, followed by hours of rehearsals. Finally, in March, the cast list for the spring show was posted. The show was *Giselle*—a tragic romance about a young woman who is betrayed by a flirtatious nobleman. After dying of heartbreak, she haunts her lover, along with the spirits of other scorned girls, forcing the men who hurt them to dance themselves to death by exhaustion. At the very bottom of the page, the final line of cast B, was my name.

A ghost.

"Check the new cast list," the receptionist, Tanya, said to the dancers as we walked into the studio.

We'd been rehearsing *Giselle* for two months when we heard that the cast list had changed; opening night was only four weeks away. Thirty dancers huddled around the bulletin board to make sure they were safe, peeling away in relief when they found their role hadn't changed. I read the list from top to bottom, then again from bottom to top. I'd memorized the former list, the first company list that had ever featured my name. This new list had one change: I was no longer on it.

I looked to the ground, walked out the front door, and got back in my mom's car.

"I quit," I told her.

And we drove away.

4

ON PATIENCE

In your infinite love you made us for yourself.

THE BOOK OF COMMON PRAYER,
"THE HOLY EUCHARIST"

SAINT LOUIS, MISSOURI

The structural strength of a wheat loaf is formed through the tension of two amino acids with opposing qualities. Gliadin likes to stretch, while glutenin wants to hold its shape. Together, they make up the protein gluten. The tension formed through gluten bonds allows the baker to shape a loaf that maintains its structure as the yeasts eat their way through the dough.

The development of gluten in dough requires time and lots of rest. As a baker kneads, she senses when the proteins are growing tired and stops to let them relax before working them anymore. Her body learns when to push and when to let go. If the dough is worked too hard, the strands will tear instead of building up more strength.

In recent years, wheat flour has become the subject of much critique. With gluten intolerance on the rise, particularly in the West, many consumers choose to cut bread out of their diet altogether. There isn't conclusive evidence for why wheat sensitivity is increasing. Some cite the industrialization of agriculture during the green revolution—the period following World War II—which altered the ways soil was treated and crops were grown. Others say modern harvesting methods are to blame, though the length of fermentation can improve the digestibility of a loaf.

The common thread through each of these is that they cut back on time. When the growth, harvest, or fermentation of wheat is rushed, the flour fails to transform fully into a digestible loaf. With a long, slow rise, however, the wheat is able to break down, releasing nutrients and flavor. Sweet and perhaps a touch tangy on the tongue—and easy on the belly, too.

I ran up the back steps of our patio one July afternoon, a month after my final ballet class. I'd finished the semester to the awkward smiles of dancers who weren't sure what to say to their colleague who had been dropped at the eleventh hour. Though I skipped all the performances of *Giselle*, I stayed in the piece my instructor choreographed for the spring recital—the one show I was not allowed to be kicked out of. In those weeks of awkward smiles and technique classes void of any drive, I'd begun to imagine what I might do with all my free time.

I leaped up every other step, and at the top of the landing, my foot slipped. Mom opened the sliding glass door to check on me.

I was splayed out flat on the hot porch, grinning. Though winded, I managed to huff out my excitement: "I got a job!"

Mom helped me to my feet while I caught my breath and told her the details. An hour earlier, I'd left for a tour of local stores, where I dropped off my one-page résumé detailing my babysitting experience. At the final stop, the Saint Louis Bread Company on Olive Road, the manager sat me down on the spot.

"Most kids don't come in with a résumé in hand," he wheezed, resting the sheet of paper on his substantial belly.

I stared back in silence, unsure why anyone would go out in search of a job without all the necessary information in hand.

"Will $7.25 an hour do?"

It was a full dollar more than Alyssa had made when she started at our local frozen custard spot, so I told him it would do. We filled out paperwork and shook hands, and he told me he'd call me soon about my schedule.

The Saint Louis Bread Company is the employer of many teenage Saint Louisans. It's not uncommon to find high schoolers rummaging through the aisles of T.J. Maxx for the standard uniform of pastel polos and khaki pants. The local chain had expanded nationally a few years before, changing its name to Panera so as not to turn off potential customers outside the shadow of our Arch. The name change didn't go over well locally, so the company committed to two separate monikers: Saint Louis Bread Company in Missouri, and Panera everywhere else.

A week later I was sitting through a full day of training. We studied the imagery of the restaurant's logo—a woman cradling a loaf like a child. We learned the Latin origins of the nationwide name; we soaked in the company's vision of a space where everyone could feel like they belonged. It was my first corporate training experience, so I hadn't yet learned to roll my eyes at company jargon about values and identity. I scribbled notes about how to handle a customer whose credit card was declined, how to correct errors in orders, how to appease angry guests.

On my first official day on the job, I was trained to work in the bakery, taking orders and serving customers bagels, muffins, and croissants. I learned the different sizes of bread—a baguette versus a demi versus a boule—as well as the various flavors we had available from day to day. I studied the texture differences for each kind of crust, prepared to answer any questions a customer might bring up.

Bread Co., the restaurant's colloquial name in Saint Louis, was famous for its donation program—or "doughnation," as the corporate handbook called it. Bakery items were prepared fresh every morning, with leftovers piled into large plastic bags to send to different charities every night. Team members were free to take a few treats home, a policy I employed quite liberally. I loaded a bag with muffins and scones for my siblings and friends, along with shards of caramelized sugar topping that fell off the cinnamon bagel for Mom.

It was the summer of sweet sixteens, of classmates with driver's licenses and the newfound ability to hang out away from the prying eyes of parents. My friends and I drove ourselves to concerts and to the mall and explored new pockets of the city together. With the influx of cash from our summer jobs and few expenses, we found our favorite coffee shops and cupcakeries. Freed from the scrutiny of artistic directors, the confines of pink mesh tights, and the time constraints of rehearsal, I tasted, for a brief moment, the joy of what my teenage years could be.

"I think I have a crush on Drew," I told my friends Hannah and Aly as we sat on Aly's bed, flipping through old issues of *Teen Vogue*.

"But you never talk to him," Aly responded.

"I don't know—I just get nervous, I guess. I don't think he notices me." I shrugged. "I just want a boyfriend so bad!"

"I have a crush on Seth," Hannah added. "He's so cute!"

Hannah and I had been friends since the first week of freshman year, when we bonded over the transition from homeschool to private school. Neither of us had dated or been kissed before, but we talked about our crushes often. We were sure this would be the summer of change.

A few months earlier we'd befriended Aly, one of the popular girls in school, and had worked our way into the cool crowd.

Like KK, Hannah had a sense of humor that drew people in. Her jokes flowed as freely as her long blonde hair, and her laughter was contagious. Everyone wanted to be her friend, and everyone knew we came as a pair. I felt safe by Hannah's side, her presence granting me permission to say whatever came to mind.

Whenever she left the room, though, I clammed up. I feared that no one else wanted me around, and my voice trembled whenever I tried to add to the conversation.

As our group of friends met up with boys, exploring one another's bodies in the backseats of their new cars, my concerns turned in a different direction.

I awoke one Saturday morning to find Alyssa sitting on her bed, right beside mine, her face stern.

"Don't go upstairs," she said.

I looked back at her, confused. It was nine o'clock. Mom never let us sleep in that late.

"Something's wrong with Mom and Dad," Alyssa added. "Mom's crying a lot, and Dad's packing a bag."

I couldn't process what she'd just said. We'd grown up learning about the lifelong covenant of marriage—divorce wasn't an option. Our parents loved each other, never withholding affection from us or from one another. They never fought—at least from what we'd seen, so there must have been some explanation for the drama unfolding upstairs.

"Your dad and I are separating for a little while," Mom told us an hour later, as we all sat together in the basement bedroom Alyssa and I shared. "He's moving into a neighbor's house this afternoon."

My siblings and I were stunned and weepy, and we processed our grief in different ways. Alyssa and I channeled our emotions into hours of TV, while Davis played airsoft wars with his friends. Emma Claire, age six, and our youngest brother, Isaiah, nearing three years old at the time, remained somewhat removed from the change. Dad came by to visit in the evenings until the younger two went to bed, approximating normalcy as best he could.

"How was work today, Kendall?" he asked as I stabbed at a crouton made from a leftover sesame loaf I'd brought home.

I shrugged, refusing to look him in the eye.

"Alyssa, you feeling ready to head off to school?"

"I guess," she said, unwilling to let on how much she wanted to be away from home. She was counting down the days until she moved to Alabama for college.

Silence.

"Daddy, look at my new tiara!" Emma Claire piped up, strings of plastic beads hanging from her wrists and neck. "Want to play dress-up with me and Isaiah after dinner?"

"Yeah!" Isaiah added, a superhero cape hanging over the back of his chair.

Alyssa locked eyes with me from across the table, as if to say, *Let's go.*

We picked up our plates and slid them into the dishwasher before descending to the basement to watch more TV.

Unsure of how to comfort me in my sadness, and perhaps a bit annoyed that my sorrow put a damper on their summer of fun, my friends began to meet up without me. They would flirt with boys at the park or give out their phone numbers at the pool.

"You don't want to give your heart away," I'd warn them when they told me about another boy who'd caught their eye. I hoped that stringent protection over our love lives would somehow save us all from the grief I was witnessing at home—or at least save me from the tides of any more change.

Whether because I was mopey or pious, the boys avoided me—which didn't really matter, because I was too shy to talk to them anyway. Instead, I pored over Bible studies and books about biblical womanhood. And I prayed that God would mold me into the woman I was meant to be—the surefire way to stable marriage at a young age, according to the literature. This hope was a balm during my parents' separation, an assurance that I would never be left in the gap this way.

On the weekend that Mom took Alyssa to Alabama for her college orientation, Dad took the rest of us to a hotel not far from home for a change of scenery. Emma Claire and Isaiah splashed in the hotel pool with Dad while Davis watched TV and I read in our room. I went to bed early, bored, wishing I were out with friends. I was awakened at midnight by a call from Hannah.

"I kissed Seth," she said, giggling into the phone. "I'm sorry, I know you're sleeping. It's just—I wanted to tell you that it happened."

"Yay," I said, trying to muster up excitement while blinking back tears.

"Go back to sleep," she responded.

When Alyssa moved away for college that fall and I returned to high school without her, I lost any bit of relational mooring that remained. Without the resistance of pliés or the weightlessness of grand allegro routines to bookend my days, I didn't know where to channel the anxious energy that permeated my body. So I ate and I fed others, and though I didn't see it as connected in any way, I prayed.

I wrote Scripture with colorful pens on scraps of paper to hang around my room—verses that reminded me of God's unchangeable nature. God's ever-present love. God's promise to answer prayer. I kept journals of notes to God about my loneliness, my anxiety, the loss of family and friends. Each page was stained by tears.

I'd hear Mom scream off the back porch to let out the pent-up stress she felt: angry that her marriage hadn't gone as planned, exhausted from caring for moody teenagers and whining toddlers on her own. Then she'd come back in and finish cooking dinner, as though nothing had happened.

I wrote a booklet of poetry for my English class, attempting to express my emotions in rhyme.

"Your writing is really good," my teacher, Ms. Zavaglia, told me after class one day. "You should keep it up. But . . . is everything okay?"

"I'm fine," I responded, not wanting to speak my sadness aloud.

Though I knew God's Word says the Spirit is a comforter, one who draws near, God seemed elusive to me. No matter how many verses I wrote on scraps of paper, my restlessness remained.

My high school, Westminster Christian Academy, didn't have locks on our lockers, which allowed students to leave notes and surprises for each other between classes. Soon after the fall semester began, it became known that I brought treats from work to share. During breaks, students would visit my locker and rummage for a snack. While it felt like my relationships were slipping through my fingers, I found that people stuck around when I shared food. I clung to the fragile sense of belonging that remained, one leftover bagel at a time.

Work provided distraction and an excuse to bow out of any social engagements I assumed I would have been left out of anyway, so I committed to as many shifts as I could. I'd rush from school to the café in time for my manager to pull the afternoon batch of baguettes from the oven. The crusts crackled behind the bagel display as I counted the money in my drawer. The flow from register to coffee bar to bagging bread had its own kind of choreography. For a few hours each afternoon, my body knew exactly what to do.

As friends came to expect my morning haul, the demands on my end-of-the-day leftover bag grew.

"Didn't know Westminster was on our donation list," an older coworker commented.

"That's a pretty heavy bag you got there," someone else said. "You sure you can carry it to your car?"

When my dad moved to the basement down the street, he moved to a new church as well, one known for its commitment to racial justice in our city—the same church Hannah had been to all her life. The congregation met at a former boarding school in Saint Louis, with the gym as its sanctuary. They sought to model the vision of the Kingdom of God in the book of Revelation—a place where every tribe, tongue, and nation worshiped together.

Made up of a mix of Saint Louis natives, refugees, and graduate students, they sang in English, French, Spanish, Swahili, and occasionally other tribal languages from around the world. The first half of every service was bilingual, with two pastors sharing the mic to make readings and announcements in English and French. Then the community split to hear a sermon in their respective language.

Since arriving in Missouri, our family had been attending a formal Presbyterian church. Mom and Dad loved that every robe and creed served a purpose in the service. The sermons were long, and the music was limited to just three hymns, which were played in the ten minutes before the service began. I loathed the stiff gatherings that failed to capture my emotion and my attention. Youth group was meant to serve as a time when the teenagers could let loose, but I was hungry for sincere worship, not just the freedom to run around. So I attended the adult Sunday school lessons instead, where at least I found the conversation stimulating.

"I need a church that captures my heart, not just my mind," Dad explained when telling us about his change in worship venue. I'd visited New City Fellowship with Hannah before Dad started attending and had begged my parents to go more often. I was enraptured by the music, by the mix of languages. God felt palpable there. With one parent now attending, I went as often as I could. In time, my mom and other siblings began attending too.

We've come this far by faith

we sang almost every week,

Leaning on the Lord
Trusting in his holy Word
He's never failed me yet.

I drank in the words of every sermon and song, praying that the Lord would carry me on in faith. I swayed and clapped and lifted my hands in rhythm with the ululations of women in the back. From time to time, a conga line would break out and the whole church would dance together in worshipful celebration.

The men and women in the congregation were no strangers to trauma, displacement, and pain, whether they'd fled violence in their home countries or faced the racial disparities that plagued Saint Louis. The pervasive evil of the world was a given, but the focus was on the God who heals and restores, the God who transforms broken systems.

Each week we ended the service by getting out of our chairs and standing in a circle around the perimeter of the gym to share Communion. The pastors would bless the elements, and then the elders would pass them around until everyone had a chance to partake. We would sing with the taste of oyster cracker still on our tongues, looking at the communion of women, men, and children from different languages and traditions who were brought together in this space.

The church was a regular recipient of another local bakery's donation program. Companion Bakery would deliver bags of their leftover bagels and loaves on Saturday nights, and on Sundays these gifts were poured onto a table at the back of the sanctuary. Companion was known for their sourdough bagels and their hand-formed loaves, which were made using old-school European methods. After the service, everyone would pick up chairs and mingle while children ran around with bread in hand, playing tag.

When Alyssa came home from college the next summer, our parents sat the five of us down.

"We're renewing our vows," Mom shared, tears in her eyes. Dad sat beside her, holding her hand. "We want to have a service in the backyard, then a big lunch with friends afterward."

Between Davis's youth camp, Alyssa's short-term mission trip, and an upcoming school trip for me, the best date for the event was only a week away. The next few days were a flurry of preparations: trips to the mall to pick out dresses and shoes, drives to the florist to select simple bouquets.

It would be easy to say that when we awoke that Saturday, the pain from the morning a year before melted away. But the truth, of course, is more complex. Just as a rushed fermentation leaves bread without flavor and hard to digest, a rushed attempt to close a difficult chapter prevents us from acknowledging its full impact. But I needed the story to be simple: the God who healed families was restoring ours. I could rest again.

I spent the rest of that summer working at Panera, as well as at a local pool with Aly and our friend Paige. We arranged to work the same lifeguard shifts as much as possible, arriving a few hours early to take kickboxing and yoga classes at the gym next door. We'd run laps and lift weights with the ease of teenagers who had few responsibilities aside from summer jobs.

Having watched our older sisters head off to college and lose touch with their high school friends, we wanted to make the most of the time that remained.

"What if we try out for swim team this fall?" Aly asked one day while we ran.

"Why not?" I responded. "That sounds fun!"

Each afternoon I switched from my royal blue bikini to khakis and a polo, working the Panera register with the lingering scent of coconut sunscreen as perfume.

"You know, we were worried about you working at the pool," Paige said, laughing, near the end of summer. "Aly and I were afraid that if you ever got a shift without us, you wouldn't speak to anyone."

I gave a half smile, not quite sure how to respond.

"But you did great!"

Our new church sparked in me a deeper craving for God's work in the world. I crafted a paper at the beginning of my senior year English class titled "I Believe in Adventure." In it, I wrote of my hunger to try new foods, to climb mountains, to travel the world. I made a goal to one day run a marathon and write a book. I wanted to drink in the fullness of God's creation and do my part to usher in God's healing.

During my ballet years, I assumed I would skip college and head straight into a professional dance career. The unknowns of the collegiate

world intimidated me—sororities, intervarsity sports, campus ministries, and dorms. I'd lived on university campuses during my summer
dance intensives, but my days were structured and the expectations
were clear. Those weeks felt like an escape from the social pressures
of school. I was worried that college would feel like an extension of
high school: I'd need to start over making friends while navigating the
unspoken social norms of the community. And if I lived there, I would
never get an escape from the spaces everyone else seemed to understand
with ease.

"You should look at Cornell," my academic advisor recommended
after I took the required standardized tests. "You can dance there, you
know. I think you'd find the rigor stimulating too."

I began looking into all that the school had to offer: a stunning
campus in a small town, its waterfalls and mountains a stark contrast
to the Midwestern suburbs I knew. Pristine dance studios and multiple
theaters. Plus an emphasis on double majors that blended unexpected
areas of study. For the first time, I got excited about the prospect of
more school.

"I can study nutrition and dance at the same time," I told my parents. "I could work with ballet schools and companies to help other
girls like me!"

I thought back to every dance instructor who had recommended
different tricks to help me to lose weight as I grew up. They'd casually
suggest I track every item that went into my body, assuring me I didn't
have an eating disorder. I was too smart for that, they said, as though
intelligence had the power to combat such a thing. But maybe I could
use that intelligence, I thought, to help others from falling into the same
trap. With a degree in dance and a more thorough understanding of
food, perhaps I could offer sounder guidance.

Though my parents were grateful I was softening to the concept of
college, they were hesitant about a campus visit. Flights from St. Louis
to Ithaca, New York, were expensive, as were hotels once we got there.
But I was adamant.

"My chances of getting in are higher if I apply for early admission," I told them. "And it's binding. So if I'm accepted, I have to go."

After submitting my application, I was told the decision letter would arrive in my inbox at 4:00 p.m. on December 11. My eighteenth birthday.

⎯⎯⎯⎯⎯

I woke up feeling confident about the email that was due to arrive that afternoon. Aly and Hannah planned to take me out to dinner after swim practice to celebrate both my birthday and my acceptance to Cornell. I was so sure God had ordered my college plans that I was all or nothing. Cornell was the only school whose application I completed. If I didn't get in, I would take a gap year, though I assumed a backup plan was unnecessary.

Halfway through swim practice, I crawled out of the pool to check my phone. I stood shivering in the locker room, thanks to a combination of nerves and the December air that was rushing in through an open door. "We're sorry . . ." was all I read before my goggles filled with tears.

My team sat waiting in the pool, ready to cheer me on. I was one of the only students from our class who had applied to an Ivy League school. When I stepped out of the locker room, I wore the same shame I'd felt two years before when I walked out of the studio after I was cut from *Giselle*. My cheeks burned with the public humiliation of everyone knowing I was both too much and not enough. I slipped into the water and finished practice in silence, preparing the speech I'd give my parents about not going to college next year.

Aly offered an awkward smile from the next lane. "You okay?" she asked. "Still want to go to dinner?"

"Yep," I responded.

When practice ended, I left without talking to anyone.

"Hannah and I will pick you up at seven," Aly yelled as I rushed out of the locker room.

I blurted out my news the moment I stepped into the house, my hair still dripping, smelling of chlorine. "I'm going to Africa," I announced.

My parents were sitting at the dining table next to a pile of envelopes and birthday gifts.

"Oh."

"I, uh . . . so I take it you heard from Cornell?" Dad asked.

"Yes." I launched into a description of what an organization called Mercy Ships was doing, telling them about a hospital ship called the MV *Africa Mercy*, which was docked off the coast of West Africa. "I'm going to apply to volunteer there," I said, as matter-of-factly as I could.

The nonprofit was headquartered in Garden Valley, Texas, just a few miles from Mineola—the small town where Dad's parents had been living since retiring from ministry ten years earlier. Nana and Big Daddy spoke highly of their experience with local Mercy Ships folks, which provided my parents enough confidence to send their teenage daughter overseas, as long as I could secure the funds for round-trip airfare and monthly cabin fees.

"Apply to one more school for next year, will you?" my dad said. "Just in case you change your mind."

Wheaton College had the shortest application of any other school on my radar, so I filled it out to please him. But I didn't want to think about college anymore. I'd tried and failed, so I decided to focus on my upcoming nautical adventure instead.

DINNER ROLLS

Whether you're going to a funeral reception or a wedding celebration, a Saturday breakfast or a post-church brunch, these rolls are perfect for every manner of church meal.

2 cups (8 ounces) flour (sprouted, all-purpose, or bread flour, or any mix of these)
1 tablespoon sugar

1½ teaspoons instant yeast
1 teaspoon kosher salt
½ cup (4 ounces) milk
1 stick (4 ounces) butter
2 eggs

1. In a large bowl, mix the flour, sugar, yeast, and salt, forming a well in the center of the bowl.
2. Warm the milk until it's just warm to the touch. Melt the butter and whisk together with the milk and eggs.
3. Pour the liquid ingredients into the well, and then mix until the dough comes together. It will be very loose at first. Continue mixing with a fair bit of force until you see glossy strands of gluten beginning to form. The full batch of dough should hold together as you mix with your hand or by spoon.
4. Let the dough rest at room temperature for 30 minutes, and then mix vigorously for 3 more minutes.
5. Pour the dough onto a floured tray, wrap in plastic wrap, and place in the refrigerator overnight.
6. After the dough has chilled overnight, divide into 6 pieces and shape into dinner rolls.
7. Preheat the oven to 325° F. Meanwhile, let the rolls rest about 30 minutes or until they slowly spring back when pressed with a finger. If you'd like, you can brush the dinner rolls with egg white.
8. Once proofed, bake the rolls for 30 minutes. After baking, let cool and enjoy!

Note: If you'd prefer to make cinnamon rolls with the dough, follow steps 1–5. After the dough has chilled overnight, lightly flour the counter and roll out the dough to an 8-inch by 12-inch rectangle. Cover the dough with 1 stick of softened butter and sprinkle generously with cinnamon and sugar. Then roll up the dough, slice it into 1-inch pieces, and place the cinnamon rolls on a baking sheet. Follow steps 7 and 8. After baking, top with a glaze made from 2 cups powdered sugar and 1 tablespoon milk.

PART 2 WATER

When water touches wheat,
an unraveling begins.
Proteins uncoil like
the truth
that once felt secure.

Like baptism,
the grain submerged
comes back to life
stronger,
transformed.

5

ON TRAVEL

Therefore let us keep the feast.

THE BOOK OF COMMON PRAYER,
"THE HOLY EUCHARIST"

COTONOU, BENIN

When the Spanish sailed into the New World, they were bothered by the lack of wheat.[1]

For much of medieval and early modern history, Europeans understood the body according to Galenic theory, which asserted that the health and temperament of a person depends on the balance of what goes into and comes out of the body. Both physical and personality characteristics were attributed to one's diet—you were, quite literally, what you ate and drank. This meant that the wheat bread and grape wine consumed in the sacrament made a person like Christ, not just in a spiritual sense but in a physical sense as well.

Based on this logic, along with Aquinas's ruling that only wheat could transubstantiate into the Body of Christ, alternative grains and starches were understood to be lacking in nutrition—inferior substitutes in a Christian diet. True humans, they believed, looked, behaved, and ate according to European norms. This also excluded poor Europeans, who relied on barley, oats, and rye as the basis of their diet.

So closely did Europeans link the eating of wheat bread and the drinking of wine to the formation of the civilized Christian that the Spanish assumed the lack of wheat in the Americas was tantamount to the lack of God's presence. Some even feared that indigenous ritu-als mirroring those of the Eucharist—eating corn cakes to become like God—were signs of the devil masquerading in the corn.[2]

When the wheat they planted thrived, the Spanish settlers inter-preted their agricultural success as a sign of divine favor over their claim to the land. Some even speculated that this new world was the location of the Garden of Eden.[3]

The first couple of weeks living on the water, you feel every swell—at least you do when your vessel is a flat-bottomed ferry repurposed into an eight-deck hospital ship. You learn that having "sea legs" is not just a turn of phrase and is in fact quite helpful in learning to walk without falling up the stairs. You sleep well, like a child rocked to sleep in a bas-sinet, though jet lag and the weariness from being in a new home might also play a role in such sound slumber.

"You stop feeling it after a while," said Christina, a sixth-grade teacher on board the *Africa Mercy*. We were eating a breakfast of yogurt and fresh mangoes, which were piled high in tubs at the end of the food line. I'd only been on board a few days, and already I'd taken to the habit of eating mango or pineapple at every meal. Christina had arrived just a few weeks earlier and already seemed at home on the sea.

After a couple of days of unpacking my belongings, meeting my seven cabinmates, and getting acquainted with the ship, I began train-ing for my new job on the sales team. While most eighteen-year-olds aboard the ship got positions in housekeeping, at the dining hall, or at the front desk, I'd managed to snag a position running the ship's shop and the café.

Starbucks had donated the beans and syrups necessary to run a "We Proudly Serve" franchise where, for fifty cents, crew members could purchase a single-shot latte poured straight into their favorite mug. Our lattes were made using shelf-stable milk that came in cardboard boxes, arriving by the pallet on bimonthly shipments from the Netherlands.

The German word for *milk* ("Milch") was printed in block letters across the top of each carton. The Americans on board, most of whom had never encountered shelf-stable milk before, were leery about its flavor, calling it "Milch" with a firm *ch* to differentiate it from what we believed to be the real thing.

The café was open for two hours each morning and three hours in the afternoon, filling in the gaps when the cafeteria was closed. We served breakfast to shift workers and second breakfast to the engineers and laborers, whose bodies required ongoing fuel. The rest of the crew, except the doctors performing surgery, the nurses who couldn't step away from their patients' beds, and the members of the sales team, took a collective half-hour break for coffee twice a day. The common area filled up with engineers, teachers, students, cooks, and housekeepers, all chatting and enjoying their respite together.

"You don't, by chance, like to bake, do you?" my boss, Cathy, asked on my first day. "I want to start selling cookies and muffins in the café. Folks miss homemade stuff like that."

My heart quickened. For months, I'd been running on adrenaline as I prepared to leave for the ship. I was eager for an adventure, to do something different from my friends. But while the adrenaline got me onto my first two planes, anxiety hit at the Charles de Gaulle airport in Paris while I waited to board my final flight into Cotonou, Benin.

In the three days since the teary voicemail I'd left for my parents, letting them know I'd made it more than halfway there, I'd been processing the weight of the seven-month commitment I'd made. There would be no trip home at Thanksgiving or Christmas, not even video calls. It would be months before I'd get another hug from Mom or a kiss from Isaiah, who was a few days shy of his fifth birthday when I left.

"Yes!" I exclaimed, with a bit too much glee. I felt a giggle form in my chest, the kind that could turn into tears of joy and relief at any moment. "Actually, uh, that's how I paid to get here."

I needed a total of $10,000 for my time on the *Africa Mercy*—$5,000 for room and board, $3,000 for airfare, and the rest for spending. I sent out support letters with my graduation announcements, asking for donations instead of gifts or cards. I sold T-shirts and hosted a poorly advertised car wash. Emma Claire and Isaiah ran a lemonade stand in our front yard: "Help our sister be a missionary in Africa," their hand-scribbled sign read.

I saved everything I made lifeguarding and teaching swimming lessons over the summer. (I'd left Panera when I joined the swim team, spending every moment I could in the water.) But a month before I was set to leave, the pool closed for the summer, the T-shirts were sold out, and I still didn't have the money I needed to buy a plane ticket home. Since I'd always found solace in a silent kitchen, I started baking late at night, after the rest of the family had gone to sleep. I measured ingredients into the mixer and made a list of ways I might earn the final bit of money.

To an outside observer, it may have appeared that I was praying or meditating to the hum of the mixer as it transformed disparate ingredients into dough. But the stillness of my body masked the worry that wrecked my mind. While I shaped the dough into loaves, I wondered if the result of my midnight baking might be the answer in itself. I crafted an email to my former teachers and some of my parents' friends: "Bake sale for my gap year in West Africa! Bread: $6, Cupcakes: $3, Cookies: $2."

"Sign me up!" Ms. Zavaglia wrote back. "I'll take a loaf of bread and a cupcake."

"Put me down for a bag of cookies!" Hannah's mom replied.

Two days later, I drove back to Westminster to deliver my bags of baked goods. It was the first week of the new academic year, and I felt liberated being back but not in school.

"Hey, can I get some cookies too?" a junior from the swim team asked when she passed me in the hall.

"Ooh! I want some!" another added.

I returned the next day with another round of baked goods, dropping off the treats in students' lockers. Each night after my family went to bed, I mixed and scooped and shaped. I'd told myself and those close to me that I was taking a gap year to figure out what I wanted to do with my life. But during those midnight bakes and midday deliveries, my dreams began to crystallize. Could I have a calling to work in a kitchen, serving God by feeding others? In just two weeks, I baked enough to buy my ticket home.

When Cathy asked me if I'd like to bake aboard the ship, it felt like God was answering my late-night, hand-shaped prayer.

I lived in an eight-berth cabin that was next door to a ten-berth room. Most of the young single women on board lived in those eighteen beds. Like me, many were in a gap year, either after high school or after college. Most had dreams of working in medicine as nurses, doctors, or occupational therapists, and they came to the ship to see what such a career could look like in this unique setting. I was one of the few who was there to have meaningful fun, with no aspirations of medicine in mind.

We hailed from homes around the world—Canada, the United States, Guatemala, Wales, the Netherlands, and South Korea. We bonded over a shared desire for adventure and serving the Lord. We stayed up late watching movies, praying in our native languages, and eating the regional sweets our families mailed to us.

I loved the mix of languages and accents on board. It felt like a taste of Pentecost, the creativity of God manifested through our differences.

The smell of fish and diesel and open fire mingled on the dock. When we walked into town, we were met by motorbikes honking and women selling fruits and plantain chips piled high in baskets on their heads. At local restaurants, we could sit down and order something to drink while our chicken was killed and cooked to order on site. On the weekends, we'd go to the beach or to the pool at Hotel du Lac. We'd drink grape-fruit sodas made with mineral water from a nearby spring and ride Land Rovers through the sand.

"How long are you here for?" a British crew member named Paul asked one day while I made his coffee.

"Until April," I shouted over the scream of steaming milk and the chatter around us.

The ship's crew was split between short-termers and long-termers—those who came for a season and those who lived on board full time. Every night a crowd gathered in the lobby to send off any crew members who were heading home. The drivers waited at the airport to pick up new folks who were arriving. Long-term crew members lived together, just two or four to a room, minimizing the turnover in their cabins. My own cabin, made up of short-termers, may as well have had a revolving door based on how often bunkmates left and new ones came.

"You should get to know the high school girls," Paul suggested, adding that he'd been the youth leader for the children of long-termers for the past three years. "Especially a gal named Emma. She needs an older friend, one who will be here a bit."

My own stay was just a few months shy of being classified as long term. After years of struggling to feel at home with friends in school, this strange world where nobody quite belonged fit me well. I loved the rhythms of working, seeing friends throughout the day, and gathering for worship multiple times a week. Though it wasn't mandatory to be a confessing Christian, the majority of crew members had evangelical roots. Communal worship and prayer were woven into the rhythms of ship life; many of our patients sang praises all day in the ward as well.

"We're holding a prayer vigil for a high-risk patient," the worship leader announced at our Thursday-night service one week. "We'd love everyone to sign up for a half-hour slot so we can keep the prayers going all day."

I signed up for a session over my lunch break, shoveling in my Marmite grilled cheese before heading to the ship's chapel. Emma had gotten me hooked on the sandwich early in our friendship, much to the chagrin of the Australian crew, who tried to sell us on Vegemite instead. I sat in the chapel, closed my eyes, and whispered a few words: "God, give the surgeons steady hands. Bring peace to the family."

Then my mind went blank.

I'd made my petition, simple and clear, and I wasn't sure what else there was to do. How could I fill half an hour with words to God? Sure, I could sing with my eyes closed and my hands lifted for hours, overcome by waves of emotion brought on by the Spirit (or at least the proper combination of guitar chords). I could take notes during sermons and read Scripture. But half an hour of prayer?

I sat in silence for a few more minutes and then journaled my emotions and worries to God—including my worry that my prayers didn't have much to do with the request at hand. I snapped the journal shut and ran back down to take over for Cathy at the café.

I was unsure about my role on the ship. Two months in, I was having fun, but my baking and coffee making felt inconsequential in the midst of all that needed to be done.

"How has your day been?" my friend Lyndsey asked during her afternoon break, chomping on a cookie I'd made. "I'm so hungry—we just unloaded a huge pallet of hospital supplies."

"Can I have a latte?" my bunkmate Chelsea added while on a break from sanitizing surgery instruments. "It's a long day—I can hardly stay awake!"

I was jealous of Lyndsey and Chelsea, whose roles had a clear connection to the ship's mission. Another bunkmate traveled with the dental clinic to remote areas to provide care; someone else worked in communications, writing stories about the patients whose lives had been impacted by the surgeries we provided. I was free to volunteer at local ministries during my off hours, but by the end of the day, I was too tired to do much else. When I didn't know how to pray for the specific needs of the people we were there to serve, I worried that I was wasting my passion for God.

"You're here to support everyone else," older crew members would tell me when I questioned my role.

I was unconvinced. I loved my time in the kitchen, but it didn't feel like real ministry—it didn't seem like I was making any perceptible difference in the world.

I'd begun to feel conflicted over the optics of our enterprise too: a massive white ship, full of mostly white people, sailing in to meet the needs of West African countries. Though we hailed from all around the world, we had the most representation from countries in Europe, America, and the Commonwealth. And here we were, headed to places still grieving the theft of their ancestors hundreds of years before.

At the same time, those whose lives were being transformed by the surgeries we provided were grateful for the care they received. A thirty-second procedure restored sight to those blinded by cataracts. Infants born with cleft palates could now smile and speak and eat. Young women left incontinent after childbirth, shunned by their communities, were healed, clothed, and welcomed back home. Face tumors shrunk. Bowed legs were straightened. Lives were made new through access to simple surgeries that were so common back home.

I wrestled with the tension of holding these two realities at the same time.

One Sunday, I visited an old Portuguese fort. The tour of Ouidah was an opportunity to hear the story of European colonization from the West African point of view. The museum documented the history of the slave trade in Benin, as well as the robust culture that existed in the area prior to the arrival of any white man's ship.

After showing us the buildings that made up the fort, our guide took us down the dirt path to the water, our feet treading over the last few paces of home that millions of people ever got to see. We passed the clay walls where men and women were separated from loved ones, divided by language to disorient them and suppress revolt. More like Babel than Pentecost, they were split up to prevent them from rebelling against their captors, who believed themselves to be acting on behalf of God.

"The white folks sang to Jesus in their chapel for an hour on Sunday, while the men and women wailed just outside," the tour guide said to our group, which was made up of two South Africans, one South Korean, one German, and me. "Wailing and waiting for the ships that would take them away."

We stood in solemn silence. There were no words to capture the grief that permeated this place.

"You think God hears the white man's stoic prayer?" he asked us with fervent eyes.

A decade after my journey through Benin, food scholars Stephen Satterfield and Jessica B. Harris took a trip to this same fort while filming the documentary *High on the Hog*. Taking off their shoes to weep and honor their ancestors, they remembered those who died before even making it onto the ship. They, too, stood in silence in the face of such grief.

In the opening episode of the series, they recount how refusal of food was the sole form of power the newly enslaved possessed. Men and women sealed their lips and refused to eat for their captors, exposing the inhumanity of the captors' ways. As Harris and Satterfield discuss this subversive resistance, I think of Jesus closing his lips to vinegar on the cross—the same Jesus those captors praised before ripping the enslaved from their homes.

"Food tells stories of where we've been, where we are, and where we're going," Satterfield says. Benin, he explains, is the place where African food and European food conjoined, building a culinary tradition that carries in itself stories of death and oppression, but also stories of new life borne out of those scars, of food that has nourished generations of descendants of both the captors and the enslaved.

The scene of Ouidah brings to mind the night Jesus gave bread to Judas just before he was betrayed, and the night he gave bread to Peter, too. It brings to mind Jesus' body: broken, whipped, and in chains, the way his death brought forth new life, his scars refashioned to make all things new.

The enslaved saw past the slabber sauce forced upon them, a slop made of palm oil, pepper, and wheat, to the Bread himself, who knew their humiliation, degradation, oppression, and pain. Their resilience birthed not just new cuisines but a church tradition that stands as testament to the resurrection power of God.

It's tempting to pretend that this evil is long behind us, to pretend that I never would have worshiped while others wailed. To pretend that my presence and the presence of our ship could dismantle generations of dehumanization, trauma, and ancestral pain. But the gospel is not a story of pretending evil doesn't permeate the world. It's the story of God's entrance into our aching humanity, teaching us what it means to be, in the words of theologian Willie Jennings, truly human and truly free.[4]

I think of the deep gift that is Holy Communion, our bodies made one in the broken bread, the resurrected Body of Jesus. Teaching us, as we eat, a little bit more about what it means to be the body of Christ in the world.

At eighteen years old, though, I didn't understand the full weight of all I was processing at this fort in Benin. Knowing enough to lament the tragedy that took place on these shores and to grieve the responsibility of my own ancestors in the faith, I rode back to our floating home in silence.

How can I spend my life just making bread? I thought. *How is that enough?*

Just before Christmas, the ship set sail from our field service in Cotonou north to the Canary Islands for the holidays, a ten-day trek that fell over my nineteenth birthday. After eating a birthday pie I'd made for myself, my friends and I received special permission to climb onto the bridge—the walkway just below the front window the sailors steered from. Without land or light to interrupt the skyline, we were encased on all sides by stars. Bioluminescent plankton lit up below us where the ship cut into the water and where dolphins swam through. I thought back to the ships that had sailed through these waters over the past four hundred years, their lower decks packed with captives. The darkness felt as if it could swallow us up, haunting in its beauty. The waters below were teeming with life, but they could pull us in with one rogue wave. The comingling of life and death, of beauty and fear were palpable.

We sat outside for an hour watching the show of lights before Lyndsey and Chelsea began to yawn.

"I've got to head to bed," Lyndsey said.

"Me, too," Chelsea added. "I hope it was a birthday to remember."

Emma and I moved from the bridge up to the eighth deck, where we sat looking out over the water each night while Emma smoked the cigarettes she'd snuck from the market before leaving town.

I'd never had a friend like Emma before. She'd regale me with stories to see how shocked I'd be, telling me about the places on the ship where she'd been felt up, about the times she'd passed out drunk. Her stories were no wilder than any typical teen's, but neither of us were typical teens: I was allergic to breaking the rules, and she'd grown up on the sea. I was drawn to her and worried about her in equal measure.

"Want a smoke?" she asked, as she did every night.

"Nope," I said. "Still no."

"Aw, come on, not even a birthday toke?"

I shook my head, to which she gave a dimpled smile. "One day I'll get you to try."

We sat in silence for a few minutes more before heading back to our rooms to go to bed.

———————

"Last box of butter," Cathy announced as she unloaded it into the cooler at the café. We were halfway through the sail, with less than two weeks until Christmas and no way to restock. "Might want to research some alternatives," she said. "People will be upset if they can't do any holiday baking."

I read up on the ways butter binds and stabilizes, the ways it shortens gluten strands. Then I typed a list of substitutes that would work for various baked goods. I attempted a batch of gingerbread men to sell in the café, subbing in applesauce and oil. Along with butter, we lacked proper cookie cutters, so I made do with a triangle, cutting slits for the arms and legs and adding a circle at the top for the head.

The substitutions caused the cookies to spread more than I expected, which also meant they baked faster and burned around the edge. By the time I pulled them from the oven, they looked more like a kindergarten art project gone wrong than a spicy holiday treat.

"You can't put those out," Emma warned me, holding back a laugh.

"Oh, yikes—what are those?" Lyndsey asked as she walked by.

Gingerbread fiasco aside, the substitution list was a hit. After the holidays, Cathy began assigning me other recipes to adapt, sending me on more deep dives into the science of baking.

"We have way too many oats in storage. Can you use them up before they get infested with weevils?"

So I got to work on an oatmeal cookie that could double as a breakfast treat.

"What can you do with this custard powder?" she asked a few weeks later.

The label was written in Dutch, so I had no idea what the package contained. After a bunkmate translated it as best she could, I got to work turning the powder into creamy fruit bars.

It was an unconventional start to my culinary education, built through Google searches, ingredient translations, and conversions between metric and American standard measurements. With each new recipe I made, I started to get a glimpse of a vocational dream. I imagined a café that doubled as a social enterprise, selling art and jewelry made by artisans from around the world. The proceeds would support refugees and immigrants the way my church back home did.

Maybe this would bring a bit of meaning to my passion for food, I thought. The pastries could be inspired by flavors and textures from around the globe. In the evenings, we could host worship services where people from diverse backgrounds sit together around tables.

I drew up plans and prayed through them all, hoping there was a way I could hold together both sides of me: the side that found joy in baking and feeding friends, and the side that wanted to make a difference in the world.

I didn't understand it then—I'm still not sure I do. But I was starting to get a glimpse of how food, like Communion, can hold together competing truths. Grief and pain permeate every inch of this world, enacted, more than I can fathom, in Jesus' name. And also: Jesus is still at work drying tears, tending wounds, setting both captors and captives free.

Baking and feeding is a simple way to step into that legacy.

It's as simple as flour and water mixed together with salt and yeast. And as complex.

6

ON LONELINESS

Lord, have mercy. Christ, have mercy. Lord, have mercy.

THE BOOK OF COMMON PRAYER,
"THE HOLY EUCHARIST"

TYLER, TEXAS

A seventeenth-century nun named Sor Juana Ines de la Cruz challenged prevailing European assumptions about wheat bread. Sor Juana was a poet, a playwright, and a theologian who lived among the Spanish elite in Mexico. Though she was shaped by her love of study, her days were filled with domestic tasks such as cooking and cleaning—helpful distractions, her bishop and confessor hoped, from intellectual work that intimidated her religious leaders.

In a short allegorical play, Sor Juana writes of an indigenous man and woman. When introduced to the Christian God by Spanish missionaries, the couple recognizes in the sacrament of Communion the God the indigenous people called "the Great God of the Seeds." They sing of a God above all other gods who becomes food so that those who eat his flesh might be cleansed of the stains on their souls. As the characters dialogue with the Spanish missionaries, they recognize together the vestiges of the Christian God already known to the indigenous people through their local bread.[1]

Through this play, Sor Juana suggests that God's presence was revealed in bread to those who didn't yet know Christ by name. When coupled with the hearing of the Word, this knowledge sparked in them a desire to know even more of the Word made manifest in the Bread.

Throughout her writing, most notably in her theological treatise *La Respuesta*, Sor Juana defends the value of theological insight crafted within domestic labor. "Had Aristotle cooked," she wrote, "he would have written a great deal more."[2] Alongside her love of intellectual study, Sor Juana felt that the connection between domestic labor and reason were intertwined, that they could work together to illuminate the knowledge of God and of God's creation.

In other words, the work of our minds is inseparable from the work of our hands and of our souls.

We rolled down the rocky drive to camp in Nana and Big Daddy's gold Toyota Corolla. From the backseat, I could see teenagers jumping out of Jeep Liberties and RAV4s featuring bumper stickers from their respective sororities (fraternity identity was not as important for the boys). No one else had their parents, let alone grandparents, by their side, but the camp was located thirty-four miles from Nana and Big Daddy's East Texas home, so they agreed to drop me off at my summer job.

The camp was a common summer destination for evangelical children across Texas. I'd come as a camper the two summers before attending Ballet Magnificat!, as well as for dozens of church retreats while in elementary school. I'd chased my youthful crushes around the Putt-Putt green at the elementary camp, and I'd learned simple choreography to Christian pop songs there. I hadn't been to the campgrounds in seven years, but when I was looking for a summer job after my first year of college, hoping to find something meaningful to do, I reminisced about those camp days and applied.

The camp was only twenty-four miles from the Mercy Ships base. It had been one year since my tearful departure from the ship. On that April day, as the Land Rover carried me down the dock toward the main road, the youth I'd befriended on the ship chased it down.

"They're like the von Trapps," Emma said, looking out the back window as she squeezed my hand. My eyes were swollen, and the tissues my shipmates had shoved at me as I descended the stairs had already dissolved into shreds.

Emma rode with me to the airport, which allowed us to draw out our goodbye and avoid the crowd of frantic hugs in the lobby. Though I was excited to see my family, I struggled with the thought of leaving Emma behind. After years of watching friends on the ship come and go, she ached for stability. I worried about her mental health and what the loss of our late-night conversations would mean for her.

The night before I departed, I took her up on her offer for a smoke. "Just one puff," I told her, reminding her that once I was home she could call me anytime.

Given my experience with the youth on the ship, I was placed at the camp for high schoolers. The camp directors claimed they wanted the youth to be counseled by college students who had a particular knack for connecting with pubescent teens.

"We lay out all the application headshots and pray over every one of them to ask God who we should hire," one of the directors shared at our first training. God always told them to hire the most gregarious applicants in the bunch, the ones with a quick wit and a personality that could command an entire room, the ones who kept up with the Christian camp fashion trends, the ones whose bodies knew how to navigate life with a certain kind of ease and humor, balancing self-deprecation with digestible doses of godly wisdom.

For some reason, this year God told them to hire me.

"Our sorority won't order any T-shirts smaller than an extra-large," a fellow counselor told the room as we unpacked our belongings in the cabin we would live in during training. I'd never seen the trend of pairing oversize T-shirts with Nike shorts before, but it appeared I was the only one here that was out of the loop. "I mean, who wears fitted T-shirts anyway?" she said with a chuckle as I unloaded my size smalls.

When I'd taken the pack of V-necks to the cashier at Target three days before, I was thrilled that I could fit into a size below my norm. Though I no longer faced pressure from artistic directors to lose weight, the desire to fit in among leaner peers hadn't gone away. I wanted to complement the slender curves I'd been working toward, but the capital awarded in this place was metered out on a different scale, one for which I had no metric as I rolled in that afternoon in late May.

During the first week of training, we were introduced to the camp's ways, which were detailed in a handbook called *The Way*. We were encouraged to pray about inconsequential decisions and to trust the camp's guidance on anything weighty. We were to pray over campers during worship each night. We were to pray about any sin or rebelliousness in our own hearts that might keep us from sensing God's work in this place or might cause us to question the standards of *The Way*. We calibrated our watches to the second so we had no excuse for being late to the flag, where we pledged our allegiance every morning. If a counselor was two seconds late, they paid penance by picking up rocks on the shores of the lake. After piling rocks into a bag for half an hour, the counselor was supposed to pour the collection right back onto the shore—obedience and improved self-discipline were the only purposes behind the task.

"We're always going to give you one thing more than you can handle," the directors told the counseling staff. "That way you're forced to rely on God."

We were taught how to redirect camper questions if they got too theological. "Just keep the main thing the main thing," the leaders reiterated throughout the week of training. The main thing, of course, being

Jesus and our obedience to him. The staff joked often about counselors from Wheaton College, who were prone to intellectualize the faith—their minds a distraction from the heart of worship.

I hadn't wanted to go to Wheaton College. After getting a taste of my career goals during my time with Mercy Ships, I was ready to start work as a baker, feeding others for the glory of God. I had a year of experience under my belt, having been part of a community that preached the gospel through actions that made an immediate, visible impact on people's lives. But I'd committed to the school even before I'd embarked on my gap year.

I'd applied just to appease my dad. Then I informed my admissions counselor that I planned to delay school for a year so he would leave me alone. He had called back to let me know that he'd secured special permission for me to defer my admission, but the paperwork had to be in by the traditional deadline of April 1.

On the night of March 31, I lay in bed unable to fall asleep. I didn't want to go, but as the minutes ticked by and I couldn't close my eyes, I knew what God was calling me to do.

"I'm going to Wheaton," I scribbled on a note to my dad. "I need you to write a deposit check. Due today." I left the note on the kitchen counter before going back to bed.

By the time I moved to the Christian liberal arts school in the suburbs of Chicago seventeen months later, I worried that the time spent in a classroom would hold me back from my calling. I was eager to practice my faith in a tangible way.

"Everyone here wants to travel and do missions kind of stuff one day," I told Emma on the phone between classes. "I already did that. Why am I here? I could be doing something important, not sitting at a desk."

"Man, that's a bummer," she replied. "I'm sorry. But I don't know, it still seems like a cool place to be. Are the people nice, at least?"

"I guess," I said with a sigh. "I just . . . I feel like I could be doing something more meaningful, you know?"

At the same time, I feared how intellectually stimulated I was. I worried that leaning into my curiosity would chip away at my passion for serving God. My shelves filled up with books on philosophy, public policy, and global health. Conversations from one course bled into the others, my literature readings somehow connecting with my courses in French and anthropology. Professors welcomed my probing questions, and my classmates sparked dialogue of similar heft.

We integrated faith into all our academic endeavors, forming a robust love for God that overflowed into a love for all of God's creation. But as my classmates basked in their first taste of freedom from parental oversight, peppering me with questions about my life abroad, I felt the increasing isolation of being interesting: someone to admire but not really know.

Struggling to connect with the women in my hall, and not quite sure where else to make friends, I spent my free time in my room on the phone with Emma, assuring her that I was there for her when her depression felt unbearable. I left my room for meals, class, and work at the campus coffee shop, but that was it.

"Most folks don't come in with this much experience," the manager told me during my interview, skimming over my résumé. "Definitely not making coffee . . . on a ship? In Africa?"

During the afternoon rush, my body slipped back into the choreography of my Bread Co. days. While dancing between the register and the espresso machine, I drowned out my worries over Emma's well-being and my desire to live overseas again.

Greet customer, swipe card, pump coffee, serve.

Greet customer, swipe card, steam milk, serve.

Greet customer, swipe card, bag bagel, serve.

Situated in the heart of the student center, the coffee shop felt similar to the Mercy Ships café, providing just enough social interaction to keep me from drowning in loneliness.

The café shared a wall with the campus bakery. When the line slowed, I poked my head inside to ask questions about the bagels and muffins they were making for the cafeteria upstairs.

"Why do you weigh the dough like that?"

"How hot do the ovens get?"

"What's the point of baking with steam?"

A few weeks into the semester, I returned home for a long weekend. Over dinner one night, I told my parents how much I hated school, then launched into a discussion about Plato's cave, sparked by my latest philosophy exam.

"Seems like the classes intrigue you at least," my dad added after we'd moved from Plato to Socrates.

I'd gained weight, and my cycle was becoming less and less predictable, so I planned a check-in with the doctor.

"I think maybe you should tell her that you deal with some anxiety and depression," my mom mentioned as I filled out the intake forms. "I wonder if that's why you don't want to be at school?"

After a consultation and blood draw, the doctor assured me she'd check in soon. Then Mom and I drove to the store to purchase a bag of flour, some sugar, and muffin trays, hoping they'd provide mooring in the midst of my despair. When it was time to return to school, I dragged my bag of baking supplies onto the bus and hugged my parents goodbye.

Four days later, I received a phone call.

"You have polycystic ovary syndrome," the doctor said. "It's pretty common, but you're lucky we caught it early. Most women find out when they can't conceive."

In addition to infertility, PCOS can cause insulin resistance, exhaustion, and depression, she explained, which meant I needed to stop eating anything that might elevate my blood sugar.

"Just stay away from bread," she warned, offering a list of nuts and seeds and beans I could eat instead.

I wept over the phone with my mom, then again with Emma. Not only was I losing the task that grounded me, I was losing my career aspiration as well.

Rather than work within these restrictions in the cafeteria, I filled my small dorm fridge with vegetables and meats from Whole Foods whenever I could catch a ride. I purchased flax seeds to grind into makeshift eggs, and flours made of anything but wheat: almonds, peanuts, coconut, black beans. I sweetened my treats with agave, which the doctor said would impact my blood sugar slowly, and ate them on my bed alone.

I'd begun attending a local church plant each Sunday known for its charismatic leanings.

"I hear there's some weird stuff that goes on there," a woman who lived on my hall whispered when I mentioned I was giving it a try. On my first Sunday there, I was taken aback by the intensity in everyone's eyes.

"We love when Wheaton students visit," a greeter told me. "You can feel the Spirit here. Not just think about God, like at school."

I nodded, grateful but a touch confused. I wanted a space where I could spread my arms and open my hands and let the tears flow. I wanted healing—for myself, for Emma, for the heaviness I saw in the world. But I liked the intellectual aspects of Wheaton. In fact, it was the only thing I liked about the school. I enjoyed debating how a Christian should respond to the injustices of the world, learning about denominational practices I'd never encountered before and how various theological movements fit within the context of history. In the evenings, when I munched on my flaxseed almond agave bread while my roommates were at their intramural games, I would sit at my desk and google questions about universal health care, speaking in tongues, and praying to saints.

At this new church, I didn't feel safe, exactly, but I was drawn to the members' surety and passion, their commitment to serving as God's agents of change in the world. I was curious, if a little scared. I continued to return, allowing myself to be swept up in the swells of worship. As much as I felt release while in the gym-turned-sanctuary, my anxieties heightened every time I stepped away. I worried that I hadn't prayed enough about watching a TV show or going to a meeting or committing to a study-abroad program, especially if I didn't hear God giving me a clear "Yes!" I was encouraged to pray for the gift of tongues, but I was terrified to give over control.

I didn't know how it would feel for the Spirit to wash over me, to utter words I couldn't comprehend. Would such an experience light the path before me or pull me under in fear? Instead, I prayed against this gift. I worried that anything I might mutter would be my own and not from God. I didn't trust myself to recognize the difference.

I ambled through the student center each day after work, checking my mailbox before turning back toward my dorm, hoping to catch a familiar face and maybe have a conversation. Handwritten signs littered the space, urging people to join the swing dancing club, the environmentalists' club, the Swedish club. Since Wheaton didn't allow Greek life or denominational campus ministries—encouraging us to develop relationships that crossed such boundaries—students were encouraged to find community through clubs instead.

One day I walked past a table marked Zoe's Feet, noticing that the tall brunette wore a T-shirt representing her ballet school back home. "Are you a dancer?" she asked when she noticed me eyeing her shirt. "I am . . . er, I was. Yeah," I murmured. "It's been a few years." "Well, we're holding auditions next week. You should come!"

She told me about the club's vision for using dance as a kind of prayer, especially for women who had come from competitive dance schools. They were concerned with beauty and good technique while valuing a range of body types. I sensed that subtle nudge like the one that had prompted me to go to Wheaton—God's firm but quiet way of saying, *You should go.*

Zoe's Feet met every Monday night in the dance studio above the school's pool. The faint scent of chlorine pervaded each rehearsal, mixed with the sweat and perfume of the half a dozen women in our crew. We turned the lights low and offered God the movements of our arms and legs, our feet bare so we could feel every crevice of the old wooden floor. While everyone else relaxed, I turned my legs out and stacked my body in perfect ballet position. I could repeat choreography given to me; I could do a dozen fouetté turns. But I couldn't free my body for improvisational work, a response to the music or the floor. I felt like I had as a little girl walking behind my friends, mouth zipped shut, afraid to do or say the wrong thing.

My muscles tensed as I held back tears. I didn't know how to use my body as prayer. I tried dancing with my eyes closed, my back turned to the mirror, attempting to shirk the ingrained rules that limited my movement. Thinking back to the Ballet Chicago pianist, I wished I could inhabit the music with similar freedom.

"I don't know why I'm here . . . at Wheaton, I mean," I'd tell the group every week after rehearsal, when we checked in about our emotional well-being. I never mentioned that night in bed, when God urged me to commit to this school. I didn't tell them about Saint Louis Ballet or the dance program at Cornell. I stayed silent about my friendship with Emma and my growing fear that she was not okay. "I guess . . . would you just pray that I understand?"

One of the dancers, Margarita, told me later that she was determined to become my friend. Each week, she invited me to have dinner, to watch a movie, or to study in her room. I brushed her off every time, she says, though a decade later, I have no memory of her attempts to reach out. What others perceived as pride, she recognized as my floundering to stay afloat. So she continued in her pursuit.

As a contemporary dancer and choreographer, Margarita seemed unaffected by rules. She was petite, with unruly curls that could not be contained by headband or scarf. With her bold colors, bold patterns, and bold movements, I saw a woman who had unlocked some kind of secret about how to live. She navigated the world neither in obedience to nor in defiance of staid laws, but rather outside of their grasp.

If I'd had the energy to pay attention to anything other than Emma or work or school, I would have recognized my need for a friendship like she was offering. But I was too lonely to even acknowledge the remedy for my isolation.

"We've got a performance booked!" our leader announced near the end of the semester. "We're performing in front of a live orchestra and choir for a Christmas show."

I hadn't performed since my final ballet recital during the spring of my sophomore year of high school. I was giddy about having another opportunity onstage. The week after Thanksgiving, our last week of classes, we spent each evening at rehearsal to perfect the piece and mark our placement. Backstage, we helped one another apply makeup and study for exams, though the adrenaline rush from the show made it difficult to concentrate.

"Want to watch *Center Stage* in my room when we get back?" Margarita asked as she helped spray my hair.

"Oh, sure!" I agreed before remembering the paper I planned to write. *I'll do it tomorrow*, I told myself.

On the trek back to our dorm, the winter's first snow began to fall. Margarita stuck out her tongue to capture the flakes. Another dancer, Kelsey, joined in. One by one we all took part. Arms out and heads back, we spun and closed our eyes as we basked in the coolness of the snow, our coats and faces soaked by melting flakes.

Just days into the summer session at camp, it became evident that God had made a mistake in recommending that the staff hire me. Innate knowledge of Southern Christian sorority norms was currency here. The subtext of *The Way* was that counselors needed to follow the rules while also moving naturally in this space. But I didn't understand that at the time. I believed the jokes cracked from the camp's stage about my mind getting in my way, so I racked it even further to figure out how to give myself over to God.

The kitchen staff had agreed to provide me with the special meals they made for kids with allergies, replacing any bread with the sprouted-grain bagels I stored in their freezer. (My doctor had green-lit the Ezekiel brand, as sprouting slowed the bread's glycemic impact.) But most days, when I slipped to the back of the kitchen to ask for my serving, I found out they'd accidentally given my food to someone else. I didn't want to make a fuss, so I went ahead and ate the same food as everyone else.

I was assigned to lifeguard duty during our daily activity hours, left alone on my elevated chair. Apart from me, the pool was staffed by the camp band. The musicians didn't quite fit with the rest of the staff either. But they were artsy and quirky, which was its own kind of cool, and at least they had each other. Watching them together, I missed my friends from Zoe's Feet.

Each night, the band played music that helped everyone feel God's presence, invoking tears in those who sensed the appropriate time to cry. During the day, they led a prayer and then a cheer before jumping cannonballs into the pool. Sometimes the splash was big enough that I was cooled by its spray.

All the counselors were invited to a weekly staff Bible study during the campers' free time, divided into small groups according to gender. One week we were studying Genesis 3. After reading about the ways Eve's hunger resulted in expulsion from the Garden, we zeroed in on the imagery of the clothes she and Adam sewed out of fig leaves to hide their shame.

"What are your fig leaves?" the leader asked the women gathered there, all dressed in extra-large pastel T-shirts that draped their petite frames, all wearing the same Nike athletic shorts, all at ease, unlike me. "What are you hiding behind? What's the sin that caused your shame?"

I knew that whatever I said would be the wrong answer; my silence was the wrong answer too. Nothing about me made sense in this place: not my diet, not my body, not my clothes. I sat hollow-eyed, lips in a firm line, wishing I could shrink back into the hidden pockets of my mind. I wanted the freedom everyone else had, and I loathed myself for longing for it.

After one week, God recommended to the camp that, instead of watching over a cabin of girls, I get stationed on work crew. I wiped down tables and took out the trash around campus after every meal. After two weeks, God recommended that they send me to a new day camp program they were implementing at a church in Dallas. I would be in charge of elementary-aged children—ones whose families' income level prohibited them from the full camp experience in the East Texas countryside. At least they could get a taste of God's love in our sanctuary takeover for a few days. I didn't want to work with children; I'd been promised cabins of teens. But I longed to please God, and also to belong, and in this place, they were one and the same. And so, stifling my disappointment, I complied.

Here in this pine-filled paradise, where God's presence flowed through the laughter and cheers of sorority girls with slender legs and long blonde hair, good Christians didn't hunger for things they couldn't eat or wish for anything more than what they'd been given. Here in this semblance of Eden, we were taught to trust and obey. Unlike Eve, good Christians didn't fall or question, "Did God really say?"

But I felt myself sinking, and my belly ached, and I just wanted to cry. After receiving the news that God told the team to send me away, I stood in the back of the crowd for worship. As the lights dimmed and the music swelled, those artsy misfit friends all together on the stage, I closed my eyes and threw out my arms and pretended I was in that mirrored room at school. I let the Spirit have control of my legs and my hips, improvising a prayer that spread out through my limbs. I jumped and turned, and for one song I didn't care what anyone thought.

Then the lights came on and I saw the smirks of the other girls.

We went to bed, and by the next morning, I was on a bus to the day camp in Dallas.

7

ON HEALING

Feed on him in your hearts by faith, with thanksgiving.

THE BOOK OF COMMON PRAYER,
"THE HOLY EUCHARIST"

On a June evening in 1514, Dominican priest Bartolomé de Las Casas sat studying Scripture in preparation for his Pentecost sermon.

"If one sacrifices ill-gotten goods, the offering is blemished," he read. "The bread of the needy is the life of the poor."[1]

The text, from the apocryphal book of Ecclesiasticus, gripped him.[2]

When Las Casas first arrived in the Americas, he participated in the violent conquest of the Caribbean. Like many of his fellow Spanish explorers, he believed he held a divine right to the land and the people who inhabited it. But the more Las Casas read, the more he was convicted by God. He went on to give up his land and free the enslaved people who lived on it, committing his life to advocating on their behalf instead. As part of his advocacy, Las Casas opposed the mass baptisms common in the New World, intended to convert indigenous peoples in large swaths and suppress uprisings against Spanish rule.

For many Christians throughout history, baptism has been believed to be efficacious regardless of whether the baptized understand what's taking place. This is liberating in its reminder that baptism is about God's work in us rather than our capacity to comprehend or respond. But in the New World, this belief served as the grounds for forced conversion. It was upheld by the assumption that native people lacked the intelligence to understand the teachings of the Christian faith.

Las Casas, on the other hand, believed that all people deserved the dignity of honoring God with their minds through study of the Christian faith. He witnessed among the natives a hunger to know God, despite the cruelty perpetrated in God's name. Rather than convert en masse, Las Casas argued for full catechesis in preparation for baptism, teaching of the history and practices of the church.

Like Sor Juana, he held together the tension of two truths: God draws us in through tangible things such as water and bread. God moves without relying on us to understand. And God sparks in us a hunger to learn more—to worship with our minds by attempting to put words to the indescribable love that draws us in.

There are some experiences a student should prepare for before embarking on a study abroad: navigating another language, for instance, or encountering strange bugs.

There are others that no amount of cross-cultural training can cover. Getting caught in a hand-carved canoe in the middle of Lake Malawi during a storm, let's say.

Or bailing water with the pottery purchased on a remote island an hour before.

Or perhaps watching the rocks on the coast inch closer while singing and praying in an attempt to calm the collective fear. (Have you ever noticed how many contemporary worship songs are about water or sinking or rain?)

I decided to spend the spring semester of my second year of college in Tanzania. I'd been itching to put my passport to use ever since I returned from the ship. Plus, the program's East African wildlife ecology course fulfilled my lab science requirement as well as two courses toward my anthropology major. In a choice between organic chemistry labs and a semester of safaris, the hippos and the lions won. More compelling than the promise of class in an open-air hut, though, was the opportunity to escape the tensions I felt between my camp/church community and my community at school.

The previous summer, as camp drew to a close, I'd been convinced that what kept me from feeling at ease at my church or among my fellow counselors was a failure to give myself over to God . . . whatever that might mean. I longed to please God, to navigate life with the freedom of the sorority girls with the oversize T-shirts and long blonde hair. But I couldn't put my finger on what held me back. I didn't want their clothes or their bodies—just their ease.

"It's the joy of the Lord!" they would say.

Maybe you heard in Sunday school that your heart is like a donut and it has a Jesus-sized hole in it that only Jesus can fill. Thirteen years after my baptism, I felt like that hole was gaping open. No amount of Bible study, no mission trips, no emotive worship could fill it in. I journaled my worries to God, always afraid I hadn't prayed enough or confessed enough or surrendered myself enough to make that hole disappear. It continued to gape: an emptiness like a punch to the gut when you realize you don't belong somewhere.

The more I gave myself over, the more unsteady I became, unable to differentiate the Spirit from my own emotion. Despite my discomfort, I felt a haunting pull toward hyperspiritual spaces. I found a sort of security in my anxiety, a sign that at least I was trying to open myself up to God's plan for me.

"Will we see you at the Mandate?" one of the counselors asked before I left camp. She was referring to the missions conference my church's network would be hosting in Texas that September. Members of sister church plants across the country were flying to Waco to pray together in Baylor's Ferrell Center arena. It was the worship event of the year: eight thousand Christians gathered to plead for God's love to spread around the world, manifesting itself through miraculous healings and prayers in tongues.

Several counselors from camp were going too—the ones who seemed to understand what it meant to surrender, so I put my summer earnings toward a plane ticket and a conference pass to attend with the group from the Wheaton church plant—some young professionals who had graduated from Wheaton a few years earlier and some folks who had moved to the Chicago suburbs to minister to intellectual teens.

It's difficult to hide the specifics of your diet when traveling with a group for four days. I told them that my restrictions weren't that big of a deal, not wanting to complicate our eating plans. "I won't feel sick if I eat the wrong thing," I told them, more worried about being a burden than about my fluctuating hormones.

On the second day, as we walked from the car to the arena, I shared, "I have PCOS. I'm trying to manage it with my diet, but I don't know if it's really working." I harbored some fears about the long-term impact of my diagnosis—the potential for infertility—but at the time I was most concerned about managing the immediate symptoms, like painful cramps with each cycle and unwanted weight gain.

"You know, I used to have ovarian cysts too," Lisa, one of the leaders from the Wheaton church, shared. "They were so big you could see them through my belly. But someone prayed and they went away."

I looked at Lisa, her face so eager, her eyes pleading for me to ask for prayer.

"Oh, wow," I responded, nervous to admit that I wanted healing, unsure if I believed God would grant such a request.

Soon we were swallowed up by the crowd of conference goers in the arena lobby. As we pushed toward our seats, I texted some counselors I knew would be there. They were all sitting together, but only the one who'd encouraged me to come responded to my texts.

"Maybe we'll see you after the next session," she wrote, though without firm plans, the chances of our running into each other in the packed arena were low.

The music began to stir, that steady build of drums and bass preparing our bodies to sense the Spirit moving. The worship director offered a prayer into the mic: "God, we just want to feel you here this morning."

We sang the same songs at each worship session, the words sinking deeper with each repetition: "You take my mourning and turn it into dancing. You take my shame, and in its place, you give me joy." I longed for joy to fill the hollowness that threatened to consume me. I raised my arms and closed my eyes, clinging to God for ballast in my emotional storm.

"Can I pray over your belly?" Lisa asked on the third day. I was uncomfortable with the attention, but something in my life needed to change, so I figured there was nothing to lose. She placed her hand on my stomach and began to pray. The others in our group noticed and gathered around, placing their hands on my shoulders and my head, echoing cries of, "Yes, Lord. Please, Lord. Heal, Lord."

I cried, believing as much as I could that this prayer would come true. *God, I believe. Help my unbelief.*

"Do you feel anything different?" one of our church leaders asked.

"Um, not really," I responded. "What am I supposed to feel?"

"Just let go of whatever you're holding on to," she said. "Let the Spirit wash over you."

We closed our eyes to pray more, but I still didn't feel the release they were expecting. Nevertheless, I hoped the prayers had made a difference in my body.

After the conference ended, I returned to Wheaton College to finish my fall semester. My next cycle lasted exactly four weeks, the most precise it had ever been—proof, I hoped, that my hormones had been healed. I frightened the cashier at Jewel-Osco with my excitement over the need for a box of tampons.

That night at dinner, I told Margarita and the rest of Zoe's Feet crew.

They were happy I was relieved, though the skepticism on their faces indicated they were a bit less sure about my miraculous healing.

My next period came about five weeks later, and the next one five or six weeks after that, as I was getting ready for the semester overseas.

We flew into Dar es Salaam, Tanzania, on a mid-January morning, a group of thirty students and seven staff from Christian colleges across the United States. For the first few days, we stayed in a resort on the coast with white sand, small cabins, and a pool in the center of the common area. We practiced Swahili. We did yoga in the atrium and read books by the sea. We drank spicy ginger soda and milky chai while getting acquainted with one another and preparing for our studies.

I embarked on the trip exhausted, afraid that everything I was running away from would follow me around the world. I'd never received a clear "Yes!" from the Lord about spending my semester abroad, but I wanted to go. When the thought arose that I might not be walking in God's will, I considered my classmates at Wheaton who navigated life with less angst. *They're fine*, I told myself, though underneath I worried I was choosing to rebel.

During the fall term, I'd taken an anthropology course on contemporary American culture, examining how race, class, gender, and religion shape our experience of the world. I was fascinated by the concept that such differences could form our knowledge of God. Though I'd experienced the beauty of intercultural communities, I'd never focused on the value these diverse experiences could contribute to theology or to church.

In the final weeks of the course, we studied worship rhythms as rituals. Our readings covered the ways liturgy—the routine of our worship—forms our understanding of God. I began questioning my physical reactions to church: the freedom I felt in worship and the fear I felt as soon as I emerged from the sanctuary. Fear of what, I wasn't sure—just the physical sensation that something about me was wrong. I began to question what it was that provoked such a feeling.

Our readings on liturgical practice excited me. The ceremony around the Eucharist, a new term to me, opened me to a deeper reverence for the bread and the wine. While I was growing up, I'd heard pastors critique liturgical churches for treating Communion as little more than rote routine. But I was beginning to see this structure as being robust enough to handle the ebbs and flows of a worshiper's emotions. Though I found myself compelled by the idea, I questioned whether I was giving in to the temptation to privilege my mind over my emotional experience of God, letting cultural theory pull me away from vibrant faith. If I let my friends at school in on this internal debate, they would tell me I was overthinking it. I didn't trust Emma to understand my struggle either—the distance between us geographically and personality-wise was making our friendship difficult to maintain. So I let the fears inhabit my mind but never spoke them aloud.

A few weeks before I was set to leave for Tanzania, a church mentor suggested I attend a workshop on prayer after church. The church would teach me how to pray in the Spirit, like the folks who had prayed for healing over me.

"You might find it really helpful before you go back to Africa," she said. "You never know what you'll encounter there."

I told her I'd consider it and then went to lunch with a friend. I was scared of what they might ask of me, in God's name. I was beginning to wonder if bold declarations of prayer were enough to force God's hand and effect change. Were we open to seeing God move in alternate ways?

"You know, Scripture tells us to test the Spirit," my mom had said to me in the car on the way to New City Fellowship just before Christmas. "Everyone else at your church seems to hear straight from God, but if they're afraid of your hesitance . . . that's not a good sign."

The night before I stepped on the first plane to Tanzania, I had a dream that I was beginning to float—pulled away by a spirit of some kind, my feet unable to root themselves to the ground. The dream repeated itself a few more times. In it, I was pulled up by the middle of my back, my head slumping over my legs, like a kitten being carried by its mama.

There was no pain or briskness to the dream; it was more of a tender taking-off. But once I was high in the air, I began to panic and pray. I awoke myself yelling to Jesus for help, wondering where I was going and what it meant. I feared the dream was a sign I was drifting away from God by considering a less charismatic approach to worship.

Now, though, I wonder if it was a promise from God to carry me to safety when I become unmoored.

It took two days for our caravan of Land Rovers and a tall green bus to make it inland to Iringa, our home for three months. The campus was built for this warm season. Small thatched *bandas* surrounded an open green, housing two students to a hut. Our classroom stood in the center of the green, a single room with a thatched roof and open sides.

We sat in class for a few hours each morning, learning the history, anthropology, and wildlife ecology of East Africa, taking regular breaks for chai, papaya, and zucchini bread. We learned Swahili during the afternoon rain, which fell every day just after lunch. Apart from counting, I never really got the language down, but I knew enough for our trips to the market, where I could haggle over the prices of jewelry, fabric, and art.

The dining tables were lined up adjacent to the open-air classroom, covered by another thatched roof without walls. The kitchen next to it housed a large wooden countertop and shelves for storing produce, eggs, and dry goods. We ran electricity for only two hours a day—late at night, just before bed—so the ovens and stoves relied on wood-fired heat with no clear temperature gauge.

Hoping those prayers for healing had stuck a few months back, I dropped my dietary regulations during my time abroad. My spiritual angst, however, followed me all the way to the East African countryside.

"You're welcome to use the oven in the cook's off-hours if you'd like," our professor Eli whispered to me one afternoon. "You can use any ingredients on hand too." The afternoon rain showers cut the midday heat, creating the temperature and humidity of a proofing box, ideal for the fermentation of bread dough. My classmate Megan and I hid away in the kitchen, kneading flour, water, salt, cinnamon, a touch of yeast, and a heaping spoonful of Blue Band margarine—the shelf-stable butter substitute the cooks kept on hand.

Our knuckles scratched against the uneven surface of the wooden countertop as we stretched and folded the sticky mass. Surrounded by flats of eggs that were still covered in warm feathers and a crooked cabinet stuffed with spices labeled in Swahili, I felt connected to home through the feel of cool flour in my palms.

Outside, the oven crackled, the scent of smoke wafting through the windows and doorways. We covered the bowl of dough with a damp cloth and sank onto the dirt floor to rest. We closed our eyes, inhaling the musty air while yellow-throated warblers chirped in the distance.

A few hours later, we pulled three cinnamon loaves out of the wood-burning stove, wrapping them in towels before our classmates saw them. We smuggled one up the hill to Eli's home, and then we took one each to our thatched-roof bandas.

That night at evening prayer—a routine that was new to me since arriving in Iringa—Eli slipped a small container of salted butter into my palm.

"That bread deserves better than Blue Band," he whispered.

I was so used to the margarine at this point that the richness of real butter surprised me. I ripped off a piece of the loaf and dipped it in the pot, willing myself to savor each chew. I hid the loaf and the butter under my bed and pulled out a book to read, but every few minutes I lost the war against the scent rising from beneath me. I'd pull out the

bread again and tear off another piece, dipping it into more of the softened spread.

It filled something in me I hadn't known was empty.

The program culminated in a ten-day homestay in a rural village. We
spent an hour each morning at our homestay family's field, pulling
weeds and eating *tunda la damu*, a tart and gooey fruit contained in a
fibrous red pod. After pruning the coffee trees (our homestay parents
only trusted us with menial tasks), we'd return to the house for donuts
and chai.

Most of the day we rested, reading in the courtyard of our mountain
retreat, watching the chickens and goats (a mama and her kid) wander
in and out of the kitchen and living room.

My homestay sisters had also struggled to pick up the language, so
our communication with the family was mediated through English-to-
Swahili dictionaries. The stilted attempts at conversation sapped our
energy, but every night, after we finished piles of sticky *ugali* (a corn
porridge), brown beans, and greens, our houseparents would pull out
their cell phones to stream a few songs. They'd prompt us to dance by
the fire where they'd cooked our dinner, joining in while the pets looked
on. We bounced our hips and shook our arms to the beat of Tanzania's
top praise songs, giggling at how awkward we all looked.

At the end of the homestay, our cohort stopped at Lake Malawi
to decompress. Our semester was coming to an end, and the faculty
wanted time for us to enjoy each other's company without the pressure
of our courses. We washed our clothes in the cool water, rinsing away
the red dirt from our homestays. We'd been hoping for a clear morning
to see the famous potters on an island nearby, known for their intricate,
hand-formed wares. The forecast called for storms every day, but on the
second day we awoke to clear skies. The boaters gave the go-ahead to
trek across the lake.

We pushed off in canoes, five people to each, laughter spreading from boat to boat. Our boater pointed to the menacing rocks on the left, so far off we almost missed them.

After an hour of rowing, we arrived on the shores to the welcoming cheers of our hosts. The potters demonstrated their process, pulling together wet clay and forming it into bowls, then carving designs and filling them with red dye. Afterward, we were free to shop for souvenirs. Our hosts treated us to lunch and ginger soda, settling the stomachs of those who'd gotten sick on the journey over.

Around noon, the sky began to turn.

"We'd better get back," the boaters warned, "or we'll be stuck."

We cut our lunch short and piled back into our small canoes. The boaters paddled with more gusto on the return, racing against the clouds overhead. Soon the waters began to swell. We laughed with that mix of adventure and fear, trying to convince ourselves that we were having fun and that we'd have a great story to tell one day.

As the rain began to beat down harder, our laughter turned to song— a prayer, a distraction, a plea. But every worship ballad that came to mind made some kind of claim about rains and waters and stormy seas. While that imagery might be calming when the storms are metaphorical, it does little to ease the fear when in a canoe battling actual waves.

"Jump out and swim," the boater yelled.

We thought he was joking, so we laughed. It wasn't funny.

Then we saw our classmates jumping from the other canoes.

"The boat's too heavy with everyone inside!" our boater shouted. "You need to swim to shore."

We leaped into the water in our jackets and skirts, tumbling with the waves, gasping for air. I squeezed my eyes shut and kicked, conserving my energy through long arm strokes. As I neared the beach, the waters grew shallow and the waves pulled with more force; I couldn't get upright on my own. I tumbled and choked before two sets of hands gripped my arms: Eli and our chaplain, pulling me to solid ground.

We got back to the campus in Iringa just in time for Easter—one last worship service before departing for home. During the service, which was drawn from the Anglican *Book of Common Prayer*, I stared at the bread on the altar. We never took Communion at my church in Wheaton. I was told later that they served it once during my years as a student: on that same Easter Sunday.

The wheat and the water, mixed together, sat heavy on my tongue. The taste lingered throughout the day as the priest's words echoed in my mind: "This is my Body, broken for you. Eat and be thankful."

8

ON FREEDOM

This is . . . the holy food and drink of new and unending life in him.

THE BOOK OF COMMON PRAYER,
"THE HOLY EUCHARIST"

"Taste and see that the Lord is good," the psalmist says of God.[1] It's a line repeated so often it risks becoming cliché.

While *taste* is understood to serve a metaphorical purpose in this verse, what if the psalmist meant that we could, quite literally, taste the goodness of God?

Theologian Angel F. Méndez Montoya writes that the words of this psalm take on a deeper meaning when read in Spanish. In the relationship between *sabor* ("taste") and *saber* ("know"), the act of tasting God and seeing God is a deeply unified act. To know God is to taste God; to taste God is to know God. To suckle at God's breast as the prophet Isaiah describes, and to feast on Christ's Body are to know God more fully with every bite.[2]

If baptism is our entrance into the Christian life, effective outside of our ability to comprehend what is taking place, then Communion is the ongoing method of drawing near to God and growing in understanding of the good promises of God. It's a tangible way of knowing God through the taste of bread lingering on our tongues.

If that taste lingers when we walk out of church—as we sit at the dining table where we eat each day—then our ordinary bread can reveal something about God too.

God is present with us through our bodies, teaching us and guiding us through our physical needs. To know God and to honor God with our bodies requires that we pay attention to the wisdom our bodies proclaim.

"You Wheaton students. You think your work only has purpose if you do it in Africa or something," the career advisor said with a laugh. She'd just finished a presentation for senior anthropology majors who were questioning what kind of job we might find after graduating with a liberal arts degree.

"I want to be a baker," I told her after she wrapped up her lecture. "I'm trying to figure out timing and next steps though."

I'd learned of a bakery/café in Uganda that provided business training for locals and served as a meeting spot for expats and missionaries in the area. It seemed like the perfect way to use my passion for baking and my passion for global missions, but I wasn't sure if I should go to culinary school before or after I partnered with the organization.

"Just be the best baker you can be right here," she said. "That's how you can serve God."

Though I didn't voice it to her, I harbored another concern aside from the longing to serve God. I'd spent the past few years learning how to live with PCOS, trying to manage my symptoms through my diet and unsure what the diagnosis would mean for my career. By the time I returned from Tanzania that summer, I'd realized the prayers over my belly had failed to lead to the desired result. My hormones were still dysregulated, and while there were medicinal options, I wanted to try to address it through diet alone.

I'd spent a few months on a raw vegan regimen, consuming only plants that had never been heated above 115 degrees Fahrenheit. I crushed flax seeds and sesame seeds, mixed them with water, and dehydrated them into loaves.

"Would you like a carrot cupcake?" I asked my high school friend Hannah and her new boyfriend during a picnic over the summer.

"Hmm, what's it made of?" Hannah asked, looking into the container skeptically.

"Oh, it's the leftover pulp from carrot juice. I blended it with honey and then pressed it into a cupcake liner."

"I think I'll pass," her boyfriend responded. "Thanks, though."

The philosophy behind the diet was that our earliest human ancestors survived off nothing but raw foods. If humans returned to this mode of eating, the forum boards and books proclaimed, our bodies would have the support they needed to heal themselves. While taking an anthropology course on human origins, I reexamined this philosophy. The evidence we studied in class suggested that the development of the human brain took off when our ancestors learned to manage fire and cook their food. As much as I experimented with legumes and dehydrated seeds, I couldn't reconcile the diet's claims. My hunger for a slice of gooey pizza could no longer prevail against the advocates who claimed that salad would fix me.

After a few months on the raw vegan diet, I'd been swayed by the advocates of a program that swung the opposite way. It was heavy on fats, animal proteins, and large quantities of fermented foods, and it only allowed vegetables that were cooked or pickled. Like most of the other diets I'd tried throughout the years, this one prohibited grains. Heal the gut and everything else will fall into place, the doctor behind the program explained.

Each week I bought a gallon of raw milk from a local farmer, which I turned into yogurt, sour cream, and butter. I scrambled eggs with deep yellow yolks, and I sweetened foods with a dip from the jar of local honey on my counter. I fermented giant heads of cabbage into sauerkraut and brewed gallons of homemade kombucha. To ensure the elimination of all toxins, I made my own shampoo, toothpaste, deodorant, and cleaning sprays.

"We're going to eliminate all chemicals from our apartment," I said in an email to Margarita, who was now my roommate, a few days before heading back to school. "I have tons of recipes for cleaning products. You on board?"

"Can we maybe talk about this a bit more when we get there?" she responded, though I later learned she was panicking inside.

I walked to the campus coffee shop each morning smelling of essential oils from my homemade household items. Every now and then, I brought experimental recipes to share with my coworkers.

"I'm attempting to make a peppermint white mocha straight from cocoa butter," I told my coworker Josh, whom I had a massive crush on.

"Do you want to try it?" I pleaded, handing him a cup. I didn't understand the art of emulsification, so the fat from the cocoa floated to the top of the mug—much like the flaxseed oil that had laced my barley green juice years before.

For some reason, he never responded well to my attempts at flirtation.

I mixed up muffins and cookies out of almond flour and pumpkin puree, but this kind of baking failed to spark joy in me. I longed for the feel of dough growing in my hands, of flour dusting my fingers as the wheat transformed. I missed baking for friends and watching the excitement spread across their faces.

"Oh, you didn't need to bring anything!" Eli said, eying my lunch box, when I arrived for a study abroad reunion at his house. "Unless you've got some of that cinnamon bread!"

"Oh, uh, no. This is my coconut yogurt and almond loaf," I responded, pulling out a mason jar and a resealable bag. "I didn't want you to have to make anything for me."

Some well-meaning friends suggested I could open a bakery one day using alternative ingredients. I'd furthered my unconventional culinary education by researching these diets, but the thought of baking this way for the rest of my life drained me.

One afternoon I wandered, zombie-like, up and down the aisles of Trader Joe's. My eyes glazed over at a box of cheese-cracker sandwiches, the kind with a powdery cheese-like substance in the middle. Delicious. Definitely not on my diet.

"Everything okay?" Margarita asked from a few feet away.

"Uh, yeah." I shook my head, trying to return to reality.

What would it be like, I thought, *to buy anything on these shelves that sounded good?* I continued to stand in the aisle, staring at the foods I'd trained myself to believe were not edible for me—plastic cartons of peanut butter cups, boxes of cereal, chips of assorted flavors. Then I turned back toward the door, put away my empty basket, and climbed into my car to wait for Margarita to finish. As I sat, tears began to form but never fell.

I was, by some standards, at my healthiest. My skin was clear, and my nails and hair were restored from the brittleness of my calorie-counting ballet days. My muscles were strong, and my periods arrived with regularity. But a deeper hunger plagued me. No matter how much I ate, I was never full.

The physical hunger paralleled the spiritual hunger that had hollowed me out in previous years.

After returning to campus the fall after my study abroad, I'd begun attending a local Anglican church. All summer, I thought of that Tanzanian Easter service, of the way the bite of bread lingered on my tongue. In that bite I'd felt more peace than I had in any other church service during my college years. My stomach churned at the thought of my previous congregation and the restlessness I felt each week as I

departed. I was hungry for the stability of the bread—my sole conces-
sion in the grain-free diet.

I felt giddy about the sip of wine, drunk straight from the chalice.
My arms craved the movements of the sign of the cross. My whole
body wanted to participate in the service—in part because it felt rebel-
lious, sipping wine while at a teetotaling school, and in part because it
grounded me. I knew what to anticipate week after week, and I knew
the purpose behind every move. Unlike the hand raising and swaying
of the communities I'd participated in before—each one with its own
unspoken norms about how to worship—the expectations here were
clear. Week after week the bread kept calling me back. The wheat, the
wine, the choreography. My body needed to be there.

The structure of an Anglican service culminates in two places: first
with the reading of the Gospel text, and second with the celebration of the
Eucharist. The rest of the service helps elevate these moments—the points
where Jesus is known as both Word and Bread. The prayers and Scripture
read at the start of the service build toward the reading of the Gospel. The
sermon illuminates the Word, carrying us on to the breaking of Bread.

"We ask the Spirit to come and fill out this structure," a member of
the church explained to me. The format wasn't a means of limiting the
Holy Spirit; it was a way to guide our human understanding. Much like
the gluten framework developed in a batch of dough, the Spirit directed
us through this structure, to help us focus our worship on God and not
ourselves.

I slept in by accident on the first Sunday of November. Rolling out of
bed, I decided to skip church rather than rush to get ready. I was pulling
the carton of eggs from the fridge and reaching for the bacon when I
sensed God telling me I should go. I pressed the thought aside, trying to
free myself from the anxiety of discerning the Holy Spirit in mundane
things. But the internal pressure grew, like this really was God and God
would not let me rest until I got dressed and in my car. So I threw on a
dress and headed to church, frustrated that I hadn't had time to shower.

I grabbed a bulletin and snuck in the back, a few minutes late. Settling into the green padded seat, I looked at the bulletin in my hands. It felt extra thick. "All Saints' Sunday," the cover read. I'd never heard of it before.

"Happy All Saints' Sunday to you!" the priest bellowed from the front of the sanctuary. "What a gift to share in baptisms on this day!"

It was my first baptism service at this church. The priest explained that the church reserved the practice for a few days each year, most notably All Saints' Day and Easter, bringing us into the same rhythms of other Christians throughout history and around the world. All Saints' is a particularly meaningful day for baptism, as it is a time set aside for remembering the full communion of saints—those who have paved the way for us in the faith.

At the priest's direction, the church turned together toward the west to condemn Satan and all his evil works. This condemnation was not frightening or forceful as it might have been at my charismatic church. It was a simple proclamation of a unified community bound by the Bread, by Christ's resurrection. We then rotated to the east and promised in unison to welcome these new members, to raise them up in the faith.

"We baptize infants because we don't believe there's ever a point when we really understand our baptism," a member of the church explained to me during a catechesis class after the service one Sunday. I'd expressed my concern over the practice—never convinced by the infant baptisms practiced at the Presbyterian churches I attended in high school. "But every time we partake of Communion," he continued, "we commit to leaning further into understanding what it means."

"As we baptize these children, we each remember our own baptism," the priest shared, lifting one of the infants like Simba.

The pastoral staff wandered up and down the aisles with palm fronds, dipping them in the water that had been blessed by the priest moments before, then sprinkling them over the congregation. As the water splashed my nose, I thought of the day my father had dunked me, of the many saints who had raised me up in the faith.

"As we celebrate the Eucharist, we affirm the promises we made and the promises made to us in our own baptism," the priest added.

It was the simplest yet most robust declaration of the Christian life I'd ever heard. I didn't need to chase after "feeling God" or discerning God's will to know that I remained within the fold. I just needed to walk forward, hands extended, and taste the Bread on my tongue, feel it slide down my throat, and let it settle into my belly. In doing so, I was binding myself to this community, and they in turn were binding themselves to me.

Just as the water navigates deeper and deeper into the grain—unlocking starches, pulling out the flavor, and building up strength—this baptism, this Bread, opens me to the holy mystery of faith, one repetition at a time.

This hunger can't possibly be good, I said to myself the Sunday after my fruitless Trader Joe's excursion, when I attempted to make another grocery store run after church. I steeled myself for the emotions that would arise when I passed the powdery cheese crackers, sure they would trigger weight gain and unwanted hormonal changes if I looked at them too long. *Is this really the best way for me to eat?*

I hated all that my body was taking from me: communal meals, the joy of eating, my future baking career.

"I think I'm going to visit a culinary school," I said to Margarita that afternoon. "I mean, I can't start yet. But maybe I should at least visit and see what to expect." I hoped another year or two of careful eating would get my body in good enough shape to reconsider a baking career.

Margarita had observed with support (if not complete understanding) the ebbs and flows of my diets and hunger over the years. "I think that's a really great idea," she encouraged me.

I emailed a French pastry school in downtown Chicago and inquired about setting up a visit. They invited me plus a friend to a demonstration on campus the following Saturday. We would learn how to make madeleines, fruit compote, and gelato, and we'd receive a bag of treats made by the school's current students. Margarita agreed to be my plus-one, so we set our alarms and caught an early-morning train into the city.

"I'm going to eat whatever they serve," I told her, trying to convince myself it was okay. "Just this once."

As we toured the school, we soaked in the scents of tempering chocolate, melting butter, and sourdough on the cusp of caramelization. We ate croissants that flaked as we spread them with cultured butter and strawberry preserves. I took notes on the ways baking powder both leavened and browned the small cakes. Our gift bags contained a box of chocolates, a loaf of sourdough, and a pot of jam, the tang of the bread rising from the bag throughout the ride home.

"I just can't believe this is bad for me," I said to Margarita as the train lurched to a stop. "I mean, theologically, I just can't believe that God would say so much about bread and then create our bodies so it's bad for us."

I valued the intention behind my dietary plan at the time: to simplify the ingredients and processes used to prepare the food I ate. But I kept tripping over the no-bread rule. Since the diet favored foods with historical roots and long fermentation, wouldn't sourdough bread be an ideal food? If humans had been living off bread for most of human history, and if the Bible records God using bread throughout, how could it be so terrible?

"I think I should at least start making sourdough," I decided.

Margarita smiled.

I drove to Whole Foods and scoured the flour aisle in search of a bag of sprouted-wheat flour. I was dipping my toes back into grains, but just in case my body revolted, I needed to make them as digestible as possible.

Figuring out the next steps after college is stressful for any young adult. Figuring out next steps while living in an evangelical community, surrounded by people who are eager to follow God's specific direction wherever God might lead, is particularly hard. My classmates and I spent our senior year fretting over God's will for our lives, assuming God's will to be a singular plan, bound up in a particular relationship, city, or job.

I had a sense that God's will was something like a puzzle. I'd been given the pieces, but I was left to put them together on my own. If I got stuck, God might offer some guidance. But since it was a good mental and spiritual exercise for me to figure out how the pieces fit together, I figured God preferred for me to solve it on my own. To complicate matters, there was no box with a picture to look at, and I didn't know what the final image would be.

In my mind, solving this puzzle was a lot like filing taxes. If you get it right, you're golden. If you get it wrong, God will ultimately work things out for your good, but you'll find yourself on an alternate route, on a detour from God's will. Thankfully God extends more grace than the IRS.

I didn't have any issues with wanting to obey God's will—I desired it with all my heart. The problem was that I just couldn't figure out what that will might be. Should I go to culinary school before or after my next trip around the world?

Similar quandaries plagued enough Wheaton seniors that our theology professor dedicated a day to discussing the topic in class.

"God tells us God's will in Scripture," he said. "It's right there in Micah 6:8. Do justice. Love mercy. Walk humbly. Want to know if you're following God's will in anything you do? Ask if you're doing those things. If you are, you're probably okay."

It was too easy.

I couldn't trust it.

I wanted God to have step-by-step directions for my life.

"Sure, sometimes God has specific things for you," the professor said after a student pushed back against his framework. "When that's the case . . . it's pretty clear."

I thought back to the sense of surety I felt about spending a gap year on the ship. I recalled the sense of awareness deep in my gut that God was asking me to commit to Wheaton against my own desire.

"Sometimes God will give you choices and let you decide what sounds best to you. Seriously, God wants you to find joy!"

This freedom ran contrary to the elusiveness I'd believed about God for so long. It couldn't be this easy. I'd grown so used to anxiety that it had become a sort of companion by now. The freedom from questioning God's will sparked its own restlessness. If I didn't focus all my energy on discerning God's next steps for me and I wasn't finding meaning in my life by working around the world, then what was left to tether me to God?

Just the wheat and the wine and the sign of the cross. My body moving along with the rhythms of my church.

I began weighing my desire to work as a baker against this metric from the prophet Micah: Could I do justice? Could I love mercy? Could I walk humbly with my hands in dough? Could I delight in the joy of feeding myself and others? Would that be enough?

A few months before graduation, my adviser assigned the graduating class in our major a project to close out the term. We were asked to design some kind of event or research project that we could develop beyond the semester's end—something that would pull together what we'd learned in school and the ways it intersected with our faith.

"You should do something on food," Margarita suggested.

I began diving into Scripture to see how it might impact my understanding of what and why we eat. With my new habit of baking sprouted-wheat sourdough bread, I started releasing myself from the burdens of the diets I'd been on over the years. I wondered if Scripture might teach us how to eat and how to care for our bodies, the environment, and the needs of our communities.

I looked at the role of food in the opening of Genesis—how a meal of forbidden food opened the first humans' eyes to the nakedness of their bodies. I read about the meal Jesus offered his followers to remind them of his presence. And I studied Revelation's imagery of a great marriage feast. When it came time to present my findings to the class, I burst with excitement.

"It's all a story of meals!" I exclaimed. "God is with us, healing us as we eat!"

———

When I returned to campus after winter break, I learned about a new café that had opened across town. Blackberry Market was all the buzz on campus. While attempting to shirk the pressure of pursuing God's will, I'd also loosened my pursuit of a perfect diet. The weight gain would be worth the peace of mind, I convinced myself. Plus, the doctor offered medicinal support if the other symptoms got too bad. *Listen to your body*, I told myself at every meal. To my surprise, my energy and overall happiness improved too.

"You should talk to the bakers," my adviser suggested on the first day of class. "See if they have a job opening."

Though most of the college students on staff at Blackberry Market worked the register and bussed tables, I brought a résumé detailing my ship experience and my culinary education via Google searches and ingredient exchanges. I convinced them I had enough knowledge to warrant a back-of-house position.

The first morning, my alarm blared at 5:00. Too excited to press snooze, I turned off my phone and quietly got dressed, careful not to wake Margarita in the bed next to my own. I climbed into my car, which was covered in a fresh blanket of snow, and drove seven minutes alongside the train tracks. When I knocked on the back door, a brunette baker let me in.

"Good morning," she said. "Are you ready to get started?"

I grinned. For years, I'd been preparing for this moment—the day baking would become my job. She showed me the binders full of recipes and led me on a quick tour of our production space before taking me to the basement, where I could store my book bag.

We mixed muffin batter in a big bowl, adding lemon zest and blueberries before scooping the mixture into tins lined with brown-paper wrapping.

I returned to the bakery three mornings a week to frost cupcakes and cinnamon rolls before heading back to campus for class. I made brownies swirled with blackberry jam, blackberry crumb bars, and cookie dough. I ate sourdough sandwiches crammed with eggs, bacon, caramelized onions, and tomato jam.

Every day a mother came to the market with her elementary-aged boy. As she waited for her coffee, the son would stand at the counter, nose pressed up against the sneeze guard. One of my fellow bakers made a snide comment every time he took his place.

"Gah, he's back again," she'd say, preparing to grab some paper towels and window spray to clean the smear he'd leave behind.

He stared at us while we rolled and sliced our cinnamon buns, mesmerized by the swift movements of our hands. I never told my coworker, but I enjoyed having him look on, seeing in his eyes the same fascination that had entranced me as a child.

When I started at Wheaton, I told myself I would never go back to school—culinary school being the lone exception. I rolled my eyes at classmates who had been planning on graduate programs since day one.

"I'm premed," some said at freshman orientation.

"I'm prelaw," others would chime in.

"I'm premed and prelaw!" the overachievers exclaimed.

"I'm never going to grad school," I would tell them all.

The night before graduation, I came home from a shift at the bakery and scrolled on my computer to avoid thinking about the goodbyes to come. I stumbled across a website for a master's degree in food studies. It was in Boston, the city my parents had just decided to move to.

A blend of history, anthropology, and culinary courses, the program probed the questions I'd been thinking about for the last several years. I had no idea such a program existed—that others wanted to study food the same way I did.

I brought my computer to the bedroom, where Margarita was packing up her things.

"I think I'm going to grad school," I told her.

She smiled. "I think that's a great idea."

SPROUTED-GRAIN SANDWICH BREAD

While sprouted flours were fairly new at the time of my college baking experiments, they're now available at most grocery stores. When this kind of flour is made, grain is sprouted the way it would to grow a new stalk. Rather than being planted, though, the sprouted kernels are dehydrated and ground into flour. The flour includes all three parts of the grain—the germ, the bran, and the endosperm—but the enzymes awakened by the sprouting process make for more tender baked goods than with whole-grain baking. The process also brings out the additional flavor and makes for a more digestible loaf.

2½ cups (10 ounces) sprouted wheat
1¼ cups (5 ounces) sprouted spelt
1½ teaspoons instant yeast
1 teaspoon kosher salt
1¾ cup (14 ounces) room-temperature water

1. In a large bowl, mix the flours, yeast, and salt. Add the water and stir by hand or with a spatula until all the flour has been hydrated. Cover with plastic wrap or a damp tea towel and let sit at room temperature for half an hour.
2. Once the dough has rested, stretch and fold it 12–20 times. The dough will be very sticky at first, but as you stretch and fold it, the texture will start to cohere.
3. Cover the dough and let it rise for 4–6 hours in the refrigerator. (Because of the cold fermentation, there's some flexibility in the rising time.)
4. When you are ready to start baking, pull out the dough and put it on the counter. Shape it into a sandwich loaf and transfer it to a loaf pan. Cover the dough and let it rest an hour and a half. In the last half hour, preheat the oven to 400°F.
5. Bake the loaf at 400°F for 35–45 minutes, until it sounds hollow when tapped or a probe thermometer reads 180°F.
6. Let the bread cool in the pan for 10 minutes, then transfer it to a cooling rack. Once it's completely cool, slice and enjoy!

PART 3 YEAST

Yeast feasts on sweetness
hidden deep inside the grain,
breathing life into the dough:

It grows.

Gas gets trapped in tension
built by proteins
locking arms:

It's community that transforms
the elements
into bread.

9

ON DEATH

Alleluia. Christ is risen. The Lord is risen indeed. Alleluia.

THE BOOK OF COMMON PRAYER,
"THE HOLY EUCHARIST"

SHERBORN, MASSACHUSETTS

Fermenting dough requires a balance of time and temperature.

If the dough ferments in too warm an environment, yeast quickly consumes all the sugar in the dough. At best the resulting bread will be bland; at worst the yeast will die early, causing the loaf to fall. With a long, cool fermentation, however, the dough acquires a robust and nuanced flavor.

Commercial yeast is available in three different forms: instant yeast, active dry yeast, and fresh yeast. Each of these forms contains the same strain, stabilized through different techniques. Once measured and mixed into the dough, these yeasts behave in much the same way.

Not all dough is leavened with commercial yeast, though. These domesticated strains were not available for purchase until the mid-twentieth century. Prior to this, most breads were leavened using the dregs left over after brewing beer or using cultures of wild yeast—both methods relying on a community of microbes that bring out a more complex taste than the single strain found in the commercial packet.

As yeast brings life to dough, I'm reminded of God's promise of resurrection. The process might be long, slow, and a bit unpredictable. But somehow, by the work of the Spirit, the sting of death makes way for new life to grow.

I used to think death was simple.

You're alive. Then your life comes to an end. Loved ones grieve—then life, though tinged with sadness, moves on.

Until Easter of 2014, I'd only grieved the death of a few pets and a great-grandmother I hardly knew. I was seven when she died, and while I don't remember the sound of her voice or the lines of her face, the scent of Easter lilies still transports me to the moment I stood with my dad next to her casket.

I found out in adulthood, of course, that death is far from simple. Oftentimes there are long hours when a loved one lies in the hospital, with death inevitable but not yet here. Those days drag on and bleed together as loved ones wait in that space between no-longer-with-us and resting-in-peace. Social media extends the liminal season even further, with the departed's most recent posts still showing up for others to see. Here, but not here; dead, but in some ways still alive.

In college, I had a professor who explained to a group of skeptical Wheaton students the value of praying to saints.

"You ask people to pray for you when they're alive, don't you?" he asked us.

"Of course!" we replied, well acquainted with the practice of sharing prayer requests.

"And as Christians, we believe that we are present with God after death, right?"

"Of course!" we cheered—this was the crux of our faith.

"So why would we stop asking someone to pray for us after they die? They're present with God—can't they intercede?"

Some students were angry at the suggestion; others, speechless. I, like most of my classmates, had always heard that the practice was unorthodox, lacking Scriptural basis. Though I wasn't yet convinced, I found the professor's argument compelling. It challenged my notion of the simplicity of death, allowing for a sense of porousness between earthly life and the life to come. Here, but not here; dead, but in some ways still alive.

Christian tradition centers on the belief that death is not the end. In the book of Genesis, death is the very beginning. The first human was created not out of thin air but out of soil infused with the breath of life—matter made up of decomposed plants, full of microbes that create the proper environment for something new to grow. When Adam and Eve ate the fruit of the forbidden tree, their lives didn't come to an immediate end, despite God's warning that if they consumed the fruit they would surely die. Rather, their eyes were opened to the presence of pain, to the presence of small deaths and disappointments that we live with to this day.

Dead and alive, all at once; broken, but teeming with beauty.

I was rushing to work when I got the email from a former shipmate who lived in Germany:

"Have you heard about Emma?" the message read.

I took a deep breath. Emma and I hadn't spoken in two years.

Her attempts to shock me had taken a dark turn just before I left for Tanzania. Every time her name popped up on caller ID, I braced myself for whatever new story she'd share. I couldn't tell the truth from her cries for attention—or at least that's how I saw it at the time. In retrospect, they were all pleas for help that I wasn't equipped to offer. My own spiritual anxiety felt like it would consume me—I didn't know how to be present for a friend who didn't want to be alive. Emma's family had moved to Texas to live at the Mercy Ships base, hoping more stability would help her as she started college. I saw her a couple of times while I was visiting my grandparents, but after a fight over the phone one day, we never spoke again.

"I can't handle this anymore," I told her. "I don't know how to be your friend."

She cried and screamed, and all I could think was that I needed to be free from the responsibility of keeping her alive. I didn't know how else to maintain boundaries between us, so I cut the relationship off.

Still, I feared the day this call would come.

"No," I responded. "What's going on?"

"She's in the ICU. Critical condition. They don't think she's going to make it."

I climbed into my blue Hyundai Sonata and drove through the winding, wooded streets of Sherborn, Massachusetts.

My parents had moved to the Boston suburbs just after my college graduation. I hadn't planned to follow them northeast, but when I'd found out about the food studies program at Boston University, I changed my mind. My life plan at once broadened and muddled. I still wanted to work as a baker, but my questions were carrying me beyond just the kitchen.

I moved into my parents' attic while I figured out my next steps. Snagging a job at a local restaurant as a pastry and line cook, I whipped chocolate mousse and spiced fruit crisps during the day, then made salads and appetizers to order once dinner service began. On Sundays I drove into the city to attend a local Anglican church plant, the rhythms of worship a balm after a week of long days at the restaurant.

Emma had about half a dozen close calls before this one, most of them during my first two years at Wheaton. But nothing could soften the news when it arrived. I wove through the woods in shock, feeling like my breath had just been knocked out of me—the pain permeating my entire body while my mind was frozen, incapable of reaction. I couldn't cry.

Is it appropriate to grieve a friend who is not yet dead, but who can no longer hear or speak? Is it appropriate to mourn someone you haven't talked to in years? How do you lament a relationship that's suffocating but also so dear? How do you hold together guilt and grief when a bit of relief is present as well?

My phone dinged again. I snuck a peek at the alert while driving, hoping for another update about Emma. This time the email was from Boston University.

"Congratulations!" the subject line read. I pulled to the side of the road. "You've been accepted to the gastronomy program, incoming class of 2014," the email said.

When a friend you're disconnected from dies, you grieve the end of potential. The potential for that person to live a full and happy life. The potential to one day reconcile your grievances. The juxtaposition of Emma's death with the unfolding of my own future—the start of my graduate academic career—knocked me out of my shock and allowed me to give in to my tears. I wept during the last ten minutes of my drive, then dried my puffy eyes to walk into work.

I hadn't realized when the restaurant hired me that I was joining a team of only men—I was the first woman they'd had in the kitchen in four years.

"No more sexual humor," my sous-chef told the team on my second day on the job. "We have a girl with us now."

"She's gotta deal if she's gonna make it in food," a cook shot back. He was angry at the reprimand. Before I arrived, everyone would have laughed at the description of his lust for the server who had just left the room.

"Kitchen people are weird," the sous-chef told me afterward. "We're misfits, a family of folks who don't fit anywhere else."

Except that I didn't fit into their family either.

I'd gotten the attention of our head chef, who appreciated my curiosity about the science of baking and my eagerness to work my way up the brigade. This attention caused the cooks to heckle me even more, convinced my curiosity and eagerness weren't the only things Chef liked.

"Hmm, not a bad butt," another cook said after I'd been there a week, lifting the back of my chef's coat while my hands were full.

I endured their antics, aware that the cooks were right about the restaurant world: this was the culture I'd chosen to join. I could take it, or I could find another career.

I was dicing rhubarb when the next email from my friend in Germany came through: "They're taking her off life support at midnight."

The finality of the situation hit me. I set down my knife and walked to the loading dock, where the rest of the crew took smoke breaks. Chef noticed, and when I didn't step back inside for a while, he came to check on me.

"You all right?" he asked, poking his head around the wall.

"My friend's dead," I replied, staring into the parking lot. "Or, well, not dead yet."

I wished I smoked so I had something to do with my hands—and an excuse to stand out there awhile longer. "They're taking her off life support tonight."

He walked over, slid down the wall to sit next to me, and let out a stream of colorful words—the ones the other cooks had been goading me to say for the past eight months.

"How close were you?"

"We haven't talked in a few years. I don't know why I'm so upset about it."

A heavy pause.

"It's not a real surprise. I mean, I've grieved before, but this time . . ." My words trailed.

"Need to go home?" he asked, though I knew he didn't mean it—we were heading into a Saturday-night service along with getting ready for a major event in New York the following week.

The event, a dinner at the James Beard House in Greenwich Village, could turn the tide of his career. It was significant for my own résumé as well. Even though I'd only just begun my pastry journey, I was already committed to doing what it took to find success in this world. I was prepared to push through my grief so I wouldn't miss out on cooking in the historic home.

"Nah, I need some kind of distraction," I said. "Hey, I got into grad school today!"

Chef huffed a small laugh—excited for me, sad for me, aware that he wasn't going to keep his budding pastry cook for long.

Emma had been gone forty-eight hours when our work team loaded up a fifteen-passenger van to drive three and a half hours south to New York City. This was my first trip to New York, though I'd been enamored with it for years, in love with any romantic comedy set there. As a teenager living in the Midwest, New York felt so far away, but I imagined myself in the shoes of each movie's lead, commanding attention as she walked the city streets. The skyline emerged as we drove south down the Hutchinson River Parkway, and once again I felt the tension of my conflicting emotions. How could Emma's life be ending just as my own life felt like it was about to begin?

We arrived at the hotel in time to unload our bags and go out to dinner before calling it a night. We were due to arrive at the James Beard House early the next morning for a full day of prep and service. That night was our one opportunity to soak up the New York restaurant world.

"Do you have plans for tonight?" Chef asked, as the rest of the line cooks discussed the bars they were planning to hit.

"Not really," I responded. "Is it cool if I go with you?"

"Don't really want to hang with the guys?" he said, chuckling, before telling me that our general manager, Phil, and Phil's wife would be joining us too. "I have reservations at six restaurants. Figured we could try to make at least three of them."

At the first stop, we ordered our drinks and skimmed the menu. I sat, silent, while the others discussed what to order.

"Anything stand out to you?" Phil asked, breaking into my thoughts. I'd been replaying my last conversation with Emma in my head—the phone call from two years before.

"Um, whatever y'all want," I said, trying to hide the fact that I didn't recognize half the words on the menu.

The plates came one after another. Earthy cheeses. Parsnips sliced into matchsticks and fried. Spring peas paired with smeared yogurt, pine nuts, and herbs. Rain pattered outside the restaurant as our check arrived.

"Guess that decides the next stop for us," Chef said. "We'll go to the place that's closest."

We arrived, soaking, to the second reservation and promptly asked for a bottle of crisp white wine. Braised short ribs and seared scallops warmed us. The rain subsided before we got our bill, which I looked over a bit more closely than the last. I downed the last sip of my wine before placing my credit card with the others, nervous about how much this night would cost me but grateful to be included.

"Kendall's ordering this time," Chef and Phil agreed when we arrived at the final location.

"No pressure!" Phil's wife joked.

I stared at the dessert menu, not wanting to let the group down. *Something fruity, something creamy, something chocolate,* I reminded myself while deciding which combination of dishes to order. *Something hot, something crunchy, something cold*—the lines Chef repeated whenever we developed desserts together. "Think of a meal like a symphony," he would say. "It's got to build and fall—you want the dishes to work together, not compete."

Chef had made a point of filling in the gaps of my culinary education, supplementing what I'd learned while swapping out ingredients during my time on the ship and at the café in college. In his eyes, I had as much to absorb about culinary culture as I needed to learn about technique.

"You should buy the Bouchon Bakery cookbook," he told me during one shift.

"Read this—you'll like it," he said, stuffing a copy of *The Pastry Chef's Companion* in my hands. For Christmas he gave me a copy of the Momofuku Milk Bar cookbook, which I read from cover to cover in a night.

After years of thinking about food in terms of what I couldn't eat, I was hungry to learn everything I could about pastries full of butter, flour, sugar, and salt. All my stringent eating regimens had done little to quell the symptoms of PCOS, apart from keeping my weight down. By this point, gaining a few pounds seemed like a small sacrifice in exchange for culinary freedom.

The morning after our restaurant crawl, Chef and I caught an early cab uptown to visit Bouchon Bakery, whose cookbook I'd worn thin from reading so many times. The warm croissant I ordered flaked, its crumbs clinging to my fingers and shirt. I closed my eyes, feeling the butter coat my mouth as we rode back to the James Beard House kitchen in time to prepare for the night ahead.

The kitchen bustled all day. I whipped up a lime semifreddo, I froze and scraped ginger granita, and I pulled out the rhubarb ribbons to ensure that none had gotten crushed in transit. Then I turned to the stove to sauté fiddleheads and complete any tasks the savory cooks had for me.

I hadn't heard of the James Beard House until I accepted the restaurant job. I didn't know about the awards show they hosted or the culture of celebrity that permeates the restaurant industry. I didn't know about the drug use and alcohol abuse that accompany many cooks on their rise to the top. I didn't know about the hardening of women who take part—learning to curse and drink like their male colleagues to prove they can cut it in this world.

I just wanted to make good bread and see the customers' delight when they ate what my hands had made. But the deeper I delved into this industry, the more enraptured I became by it. The sensuality. The challenge. The scandal. The drive.

Most of the cooks I worked with met up at a bar at the end of their shift, coming down from the adrenaline high of a night on the line by downing a few beers before bed. I preferred to recover at home on my own, reading or watching TV.

One evening, soon after starting the job, I found a series of TED talks about food. Peter Reinhart, a renowned bread baker and cookbook author, gave a lecture about the cycle of death and life involved in the formation of any loaf. He spoke about the death of the wheat, ground into flour and then mixed with water. He marveled at the yeast, filling the dough with new life, flavoring and strengthening it.

"The yeast, whose mission it has been up till now to raise the dough, to enliven it, to vivify it, in order to complete its mission . . . has to give up its life." In this final transformation from dough to bread, Reinhart says, the dough "faces one more death in order to become the staff of life and feed the world."[1]

As I listened to his lecture, I felt as though I were listening to a sermon, the gospel proclaimed in every line. Bread holds, in each bite, this porousness between death and life.

Two weeks before we left for New York—before I knew I'd be grieving Emma's death—I'd asked permission from my boss to stay an extra day so I could sightsee on my own. I meandered through the city, filling my backpack with cake truffles from Milk Bar, a passion fruit napoleon from Payard Patisserie in the basement of the Plaza Hotel, and a loaf of sourdough and a chocolate chip cookie from Amy's Bread in Chelsea Market.

I was wandering the aisles of Eataly, examining bags of dried pasta, when my friend emailed to say that Emma's funeral date had been set. It would be in three days, the day before Palm Sunday. The service would be held at a church down the road from the Mercy Ships base.

I hid between racks of tomato sauce to look up plane tickets. It would cost five hundred dollars to fly to Dallas with forty-eight hours' notice. That was as much as I made in a week, before taxes—but I needed to go.

By midafternoon, I was tired of sightseeing. The dream of New York had been drained of its magic in the shadow of my grief.

I stepped off the train just south of Times Square, willing myself to walk the rest of the way to the bus, willing myself to love this city I'd dreamed of for so long. But the bustle of people caused a pit of sadness to well within me. I was surrounded by people, hundreds of commuters and tourists smashed into a few square blocks. But not one of them knew the grief I carried—the friendship that had ended without the chance for reconciliation or even a goodbye.

I was there but not there. Not alone but completely unknown.

The liturgical calendar is a method of journeying through each year mirroring the life of Christ. It begins with the season of Advent, four weeks before Christmas. After twelve days of Christmas and the celebration of Epiphany, it shifts into a brief period called Ordinary Time before Lent, Holy Week, and Easter—a fifty-day celebration of Christ's resurrection. Pentecost, the birthday of the church, makes way for the second period of Ordinary Time, an extended season of remembering the role of the church in carrying on Christ's good news.

As we journey through these rhythms year after year—the highs and lows, the periods of fasting and feasting—we are brought into a deeper understanding of Christ's work in this world. The repetition deepens our understanding of the season, drawing us further in each time, like a baker slowly learning the needs and rhythms of her bread.

Holy Week—the week between Palm Sunday and Easter—marks the drama of Christ's final days. Maundy Thursday celebrates the meal Jesus shared with his disciples in the Upper Room. Good Friday grieves Jesus' horrific death. On Holy Saturday, the church stands vigil in anticipation of Christ's resurrection, remembering the sadness and fear that overtook his disciples that day.

The Easter Vigil service begins late in the evening, continuing into the early hours of Easter morning. Congregants enter the sanctuary in silence and darkness, sitting in grief over Jesus' death. Then the lights slowly brighten as the story of salvation is read from portions of Scripture, from the Old Testament to the Gospels.

Each reading is accompanied by a dance, a poem, a song, or a piece of art designed for the service. It's a reminder that our faith is gleaned not just through reading but through the process of creating together in community.

As the clock nears midnight, the lights burst on and the crowd shouts, "Alleluia!" while ringing bells and jingling keys, celebrating the risen Lord. The celebration carries on with a feast of sweets plus more baptisms and songs that continue until the participants can no longer stay awake.

I'd attended only one Easter vigil—the year before, at my Anglican church in Wheaton. I'd wept through much of the service, transfixed by the ways this rhythm connected us with generations of Christians who have come before us.

My new church in Boston was full of artists and creative people, and all year I'd heard about how meaningful the vigil was. I had planned to take time off work over Easter weekend. With Saturdays being the busiest night for a restaurant, I could only ask off for special occasions. But with my last-minute weekend trip to Texas, I would have to work instead.

The purpose of the Easter vigil is to carry Christians through the grief of death into the hope of resurrection. The bread and hospitality shared on Maundy Thursday make way for the lamentation of Good Friday. In this liminal space, Holy Saturday readies us for celebration.

Though I wasn't able to journey through Holy Week at the designated services that year, in the days between Emma's death and Easter, my church created a personal Holy Week of sorts for me. The night before I caught my flight to Dallas (the Thursday before the Maundy Thursday meal), my friend Kayla made her couch into a bed. With such an early flight, I would have struggled to make it from my parents' house in the suburbs to the airport in time, so she invited me to stay at her apartment. She even prepared a taxi to pick me up at 4:00 a.m. When I woke up, I found a box of pastries from a local café on the coffee table, waiting for me.

"Praying for you and holding your grief, friend," the note said.

I shoved the box into my backpack before heading to the waiting cab. Grief had squelched my appetite; still, the presence of the pastries was a balm, a sign of the friends who were lamenting with me. It was a makeshift Maundy Thursday show of hospitality.

When I landed at the airport in Dallas, I picked up my rental car and drove to the arrivals gate to wait for Emma's youth group friends, who were flying in from Germany, Canada, and around the United States.

"Is it weird that I'm a little bit excited about this reunion?" one of them asked as she climbed into the backseat.

We hadn't all been together since they'd chased the Land Rover down the dock with Emma and me inside. "It's weird to be a little happy while I'm this sad."

We chattered on the drive, reminiscing about Emma's antics and catching up on one another's studies and jobs. The car quieted as we turned into the funeral home, the reality hitting us about why we were there. I parked and turned off the car. Silence, save a sniffle or two.

"I've got packs of tissues," I whispered before unclipping my seat belt.

We slipped into the back pew as hymns played from speakers overhead. We took turns walking in pairs to the casket to say goodbye, holding hands to support one another in our grief. I returned to my seat, shredded tissue in hand, as the music shifted. *How deep the Father's love for us,* I sang in my mind. *How vast beyond all measure.*

I thought back to the nights Emma and I had sat on the eighth deck, overlooking the sea. From time to time, Emma had brought her guitar so we could play and sing, and this song always made it into the rotation.

An image floated to mind as I hummed to the tune. Not in a terrifying way, like the dreams and visions I was told to pray for in my days at the charismatic church. This felt like a gentle gift from a comforting God: I saw Emma singing at Jesus' feet, with a lightness to her that I'd never seen before.

I held on to the dichotomy as the familiar melody pulsed through the room. As a community, we grieved the loss of our loved one together. At the same time, I clung to this picture of resurrection—of pain turned to joy at Jesus' feet.

Folks from my church in Boston reached out to me throughout the weekend and in the following days, sending emails full of prayers and texts with lines of Scripture. Like the readings of the Easter Vigil service, their reminders of Christ's life-giving love pulled me toward the light.

By Easter Sunday, when I slid into the pew after a short brunch shift at work, stinking of old dishwater and onions and stale coffee, my community surrounded me to offer prayers and quick hugs. I sang of Jesus' resurrection with the image of Emma's joy in my mind and the love of this community all around.

Death is far from simple. And yet, somehow, through its pain, we also taste the goodness of life.

10

ON FRIENDSHIP

You have fed us with spiritual food in the Sacrament of his Body.

THE BOOK OF COMMON PRAYER,
"THE HOLY EUCHARIST"

A culture of wild yeasts, known by many as a sourdough starter, contains a balance of both yeasts and bacteria. While breads made with commercial yeast are leavened and transformed primarily through a yeast fermentation, breads made with sourdough undergo both yeast and bacterial change.

The sourdough starter is developed by mixing flour and water and letting it sit for a period of time. The yeasts, along with the bacteria present in the air, in the flour, and on the utensils used for mixing, populate and transform the dough, developing a culture that can be maintained.

A group of ecologists studied the microbial makeup of sourdough starters and their relationship to the hands of the bakers that maintained them. The researchers found that the microbiome of a baker's hands matched the microbiome of his or her starter. Whether the hands inform the starter or the starter informs the hands remains unknown. It's likely that to a certain extent they inform each other—and that the resulting loaves inform the microbial makeup of their eaters as well.[1] While the yeasts don't live through the baking process, fibers called prebiotics do. The resulting bread becomes food for the beneficial bacteria inside the eater.

The line between bread and body is more porous than we might expect. While the Spanish conquistadors might have been misled in their assumption that wheat forms the proper Christian Body, they weren't wrong in their understanding that bread and the body are closely intertwined. When Jesus said that the breaking of bread transforms us into one body, he spoke both spiritual and ecological truth.

The cursor on my computer screen blinked as I stared out the window, watching boats bob in the harbor. It was the Wednesday of Holy Week, 2015. My day off. The small beach towns lining Boston's North Shore are full of coffee shops that sit close to empty in the off-season.

My favorite, in the town of Rockport, has a full wall of windows overlooking a small bay. From my post at a back table, I wrote papers for grad school while listening to seagulls caw at the lobster traps stacked high along the edge of the dock.

That day, I was working on a final paper for a class called "Food and the Senses." The course included readings on neurogastronomy, which explores the impact of the brain and the senses on the way we experience food. We read articles from the field of human geography, examining how our bodies glean information that helps us make sense of the world.

We discussed our familial, cultural, and individual relationships to eating, each with a story of connection or disconnection through food. We probed our experiences of getting to know others through the intimate, tactile relationships that are shaped around the table—both the times that created positive bonds and the times those relationships have been awkward or harmful.

I was enraptured by the breadth of interdisciplinary research that corroborated a fact I'd long known to be true: the mundane task of eating, of meeting nutritional needs, holds the capacity to shape our identity while meeting our relational needs as well.

We used the term *bodily knowledge* to explain this phenomenon—the idea that our arms and hands and bellies know certain truths we can't grasp fully with the mind. Food leads us "beyond that which can be said, seen, or heard to that which is felt and is sometimes inarticulable," says Jennifer Brady, a scholar whose research focuses on sensory knowledge.[2]

Not only did the premise put words to my positive and negative experiences with food and eating; it made sense of my experience of faith as well. God's presence had been revealed to me so often through sensory engagement with the material world—through dance and breadmaking, through genuflections and signs of the cross. The more I dug into readings on bodily knowledge, the more I recognized that this way of communing with God was not unique or special to me, but was a central aspect of God's design for humanity.

The concept of bodily knowledge isn't foreign to Christianity; it's the very premise of liturgy—the idea that our words and actions and communal movements shape and form us. But I'd never heard the concept of bodily knowledge applied to theology. *If our tongues and taste buds and sense of touch are valuable sites of learning and knowing,* I wondered, *wouldn't they also be valuable means of drawing into a deeper understanding of God?*

While planning my final paper, I had a flood of ideas about how to carry this research even further. Was this bodily knowledge, gleaned through cooking and sharing food, the reason Jesus offered his followers a meal of bread and wine? Perhaps it's not so different from the baker who is shaped by the microbial makeup of her sourdough. What if the bread we eat in Communion shapes the body of the church—not just in a spiritual sense, but in a physical sense, too?

I was excited about the possibilities for future research and writing. But on this Holy Week Wednesday, I had no words to write. I just couldn't put my finger on why.

With the James Beard dinner on my résumé from the year before, I'd accepted a job at Sofra Bakery and moved out of my parents' house. Sofra was an Eastern Mediterranean café just outside Harvard Square, known for its unexpected use of spices.

"You should try Maura Kilpatrick's desserts," Phil, the manager at my former restaurant, told me one evening after handing me a cookbook from Sofra's sister restaurant, Oleana. "Learn from other women in the field. It'll be encouraging, I think. Plus, her pastries are the bomb."

The following week Kayla and I went to Sofra to see what he meant. We pulled apart the layers of a cardamom morning bun, our fingers dripping in butter and orange blossom icing.

"I think this is the best thing I've ever eaten," I said with my eyes closed, after we moved on to the sesame caramel cashew bite. "I have to learn here."

As soon as I got home, I emailed Maura to introduce myself and ask if I could shadow her once a week. For the next two months, I spent my day off working a 5 a.m. shift for free, peppering the baker who trained me with questions and scribbling her answers in a green notebook.

I soon learned that Sofra was committed to training their bakers well, creating a team of teachers who understood the inner workings of each kind of dough and who could go on to run their own pastry operations one day.

When a full-time position became available, Maura offered the spot to me. I was excited to trade my late-night shifts for early mornings, hoping for some freedom on the weekends to spend with friends.

After connecting with two other young, single women through a church housing forum—Emily, an architect fresh out of school, and Gabrielle, a writer, project manager, and Renaissance woman (who actually majored in Renaissance studies)—I moved into a sun-drenched apartment in Union Square, which we named *Chez Heureuse*. The happy home. We decorated the house together with the shared desire for a space that would build community, a place where we could eat together and pray together, a place to laugh and cry.

"Kendall. You should apply for this job," Gabrielle said one day, rushing into the kitchen. She'd found a listing for a contributing editor at a local food publication. They were looking for someone to cover Boston's restaurant news.

"I like my job, G.," I said, grabbing three wineglasses from the cabinet.

"I know, but you just never know," she said, digging the corkscrew into a bottle of Cabernet. "The application process is good for you. Just give it a try—this job is totally your thing."

We slid to the ground, my back leaning against the fridge and hers against the oven. By the time Emily joined us, sliding down in front of the kitchen sink, Gabrielle had convinced me that at the very least, composing a cover letter would help me clarify my career goals.

With that decided, we moved on to help Emily process her graduate school applications. These kitchen floor catch-ups had become a regular occurrence in our home, as we dreamed together about what our futures might hold.

I'd been at Sofra for close to a year, gathering with a crew of bakers around the wooden workbench before the sun rose and before the bus system awoke for the day. A five-foot-tall mixer droned to my right as I weighed flour, butter, yeast, and salt into plastic bins every morning.

Each baker was given a list to accomplish before the workday was through—one baker to operate the mixer, one to complete tasks on the stove, one to watch over the oven, and one to oversee the sheeter downstairs—a machine that rolled dough into progressively thinner layers to create uniform croissants, pie crusts, crackers, and more. As the night turned into morning, we would sip coffee and snack on spanakopita and carrot feta biscuits left over from the day before while the café began to fill up around us—first with baristas and cashiers, then with customers eager for a sesame latte before they hopped on a bus into Boston, and finally the savory cooks preparing for lunch.

With our hands busy weighing and shaping, we had hours each day to talk around that wooden table—about food, about family, about bad dates.

"So, this guy told me he's a sales rep for Cabot cheese," I told them the morning after a first date. "I was excited because he must love food."

"Ooh, sounds like a great fit!" the pastry sous-chef exclaimed.

"I asked him his favorite kind of cheese and added that I'm a fan of Cabot's clothbound cheddar."

"Ah, great choice," another baker added.

"Then he said, 'Oh, I only like cheese when it's melted on things. Like pizza or nachos."

"What?" the bakers yelled in unison.

"He's never even tried the cheese he sells!"

My dating life hadn't improved much since high school: I'd had a string of crushes, none of whom returned my interest. Some were kind in their dismissal, while others left me ashamed over expressing my feelings at all.

I couldn't help but wonder if my body played a part in their lack of interest. Though I felt good about my relationship to food, my ability to listen to the needs of my body, and my capacity for finding equal joy in roasted vegetables, fresh sourdough, and the sweets I made at work, this contentment brought with it extra weight.

At the encouragement of my roommates, I was pushing past the fear of rejection that grew along with my body by planning dates with men I met online. The morning bakers' table recaps helped boost my confidence.

In contrast to the previous restaurant I'd worked at, most of the kitchen staff at Sofra, including the chef and the pastry chef, were women. The environment was one of collaboration and support. My coworkers were confident in their culinary skills—every year the café was nominated for local and national awards—but the staff's love for food wasn't precious. It was founded on a true enjoyment of all delightful things.

"We should have a Costco party sometime," one of the bakers suggested while layering baklava. "Like a potluck where everyone brings their favorite Costco dish."

"Ooh, I'm bringing the pot pie!" our pastry sous-chef said. "It's so good. I'm serious."

Conversation turned from Costco's best dishes to a new restaurant that had just opened in the Back Bay, and then to a list of favorite pastry spots in Asheville, North Carolina, and New York City. Our uniting love was food, sensorial delight.

It was the life I'd dreamed of since my visit to Great Harvest two decades before. Every so often the reality of the fulfillment of this dream came over me. I would pause, looking down at my hands kneading dough, considering my apron and my shiny black clogs dusted in flour and the pink bandana tying back my hair.

I loved it. Yet something was missing.

"I just feel like I need to keep moving forward," I told a church leader at our women's retreat that spring.

We'd gathered at a Benedictine abbey to share a potluck breakfast, where I'd contributed a braided loaf of brown-butter bread stuffed with scrambled eggs, bacon, caramelized onions, and melted leeks.

As the women took turns walking through the line and filling up their plates, I heard them asking, "Did Kendall bring this one?"

"What does that mean to you, to move forward?" she probed.

"I don't really know," I responded. "I'm trying to figure that out."

Working in a kitchen full of teachers, I was learning about the science of chocolate, sugar, and flour. I was finding out how to balance acid, salt, and fat. Two nights a week I attended class at Boston University, and on long weekends I drove to New York City for short apprenticeships, like the one that helped secure my Sofra position. I shadowed the bakers at Momofuku Milk Bar and the recipe developers at Food52. The sensuality, the intensity, and the constant pursuit of good flavor exhilarated and exhausted me.

When I was assigned to the sheeter, downstairs on my own, I'd process ideas for articles about bread and meals and the ways they were shaping my faith. I'd scribble notes on parchment until I could parse out the thoughts further at the keyboard.

I applied for scholarships, fellowships, internships, and editorial positions—all in search of some unrecognizable goal. I didn't know what it was I was trying to achieve; I just knew I wasn't there yet.

As I drove home from the coffee shop on Wednesday of Holy Week, I felt an unease that I couldn't pin down. I overthought a text from a friend, frustrated by the words she didn't say and wondering if she meant more than she said. I overthought a conversation I'd had with a roommate three days before, angry without knowing why. I overthought an interaction with my mom, frustrated for reasons I couldn't understand.

Then I began to cry. The tears seemed to come from nowhere, and I couldn't bring them to an end. I racked my brain for answers, picturing a calendar in my mind so I could count back the weeks to track my irregular cycle.

It was April 1.

This Sunday would be April 5.

Good Friday would mark one year since depression overtook Emma's will to live.

Holy Saturday would mark one year since I received those two emails: the one that set my future on a new course and the one that informed me that Emma's potential future had come to an end.

And Easter, that resurrection day, would mark one year without Emma's presence gracing this world.

From my studies, I knew that our bodies hold on to events we forget, tracking dates and anniversaries for us when we don't have the bandwidth to consciously remember them. My body seemed to be holding on to the grief of that goodbye. One year later, my life felt open before me, but I was paralyzed by the possibilities.

"Hey friends, can y'all pray for me this week/weekend?" I texted my small group at church. "It's the anniversary of Emma's death and . . . it's hitting me harder than I expected."

"Sure thing!" someone wrote back.

"Love you," another added.

On Friday, my body began to feel weak as I watched two members of the church strip the altar. I attributed my weariness to the tears I'd shed in the days before.

On Saturday, I woke up ready to bake treats for the celebration following the Easter vigil. As I started moving through my kitchen, though, I realized that the weakness I'd felt the night before was now accompanied by congestion and a cough.

Determined not to miss the vigil a second year, I loaded up on DayQuil and got to baking. I mixed up a batch of dough and a feta-and-parsley filling, then shaped the stuffed rolls to look like roses.

I took breaks along with my bread, resting my own body while the dough relaxed and grew. My congestion was worsening, but I couldn't bear to be alone the whole day.

Late in the afternoon, I packed up the bread roses and headed out for the service.

The friends I'd texted surrounded me in the pews—some on either side, some in front, and some behind, all aware of the weightiness of this day—in the broader Church, and also for me. I worked my way through the tissues in my bag during the readings and artistic performances. As the time to celebrate Christ's resurrection neared, my tears began to fall.

"Oh death, where is your sting? Oh hell, where is your victory?" we sang just before the lights turned on. "Oh, Church, come stand in the light. Our God is not dead, he's alive, he's alive!"

Surrounded by friends, their hands gracing my shoulders, I wept as I remembered and grieved the friend I'd lost. Tears streaming down my cheeks, I clung to these words. I allowed myself to soak in the sweet relationship between death and life.

I could hardly open my eyes—the mixture of unknown gunk and

swollen eyelids made it difficult to see, and my foggy contacts didn't help. I felt terrible, I looked terrible, and I probably should have been resting my body in bed. But surrounded by a community formed through our weekly meal of bread and wine, I knew I was held in love.

When I was nineteen, just after returning home from the ship, I'd applied for a job at Great Harvest. I felt ready to begin my baking career, and it seemed fitting to start in the place that first sparked my dream. I bounded into the store, application in hand, and the manager sat me down. He told me about the early hours and the low pay, about how most of his bakers believed it was worth it for the joy of what they did.

"We have one person here who went to culinary school, but I think it's better not to go," he told me. "Makes you think you know everything, but your hands don't know anything yet."

I went home and mulled over his words. I'd wanted work that would mean something—a summer job that left an impact on the world. I didn't understand how bread making fit with this dream, and I wasn't sure I could handle the early morning baking quite yet. When he called two days later to offer me the position, I turned him down, accepting a job watching preschoolers at the YMCA instead.

I've long wondered what would have happened if I'd accepted that Great Harvest job. Would God have met me via bodily knowledge over the course of a baking career, without my unraveling at camp, at church, at school? Or would my passion for bread have suffocated as a result of jumping into the profession before I was ready?

In the same way, I wonder what would have changed if I had sought peace in that season of working at Sofra. Was that restlessness just my own perpetual anxiety? Or was it possible that this was God's method of pushing me deeper, letting me examine my relationship with bread and the Bread himself?

In retrospect, I can see that I was wrestling against the dynamics that had long plagued me: even though I had achieved the rhythms I'd always dreamed of, I wasn't satisfied with a life that failed to integrate both my body and my brain. I didn't want to just bake. And I didn't want to just study. I didn't even want to bake and study at the same time. Like Sor Juana, I wanted the work of each to support and build on the other—the baking driving my writing, and my studies shaping the very foods I chose to make. At the time, though, all I could focus on was the fact that I wasn't settled. I couldn't stop hunting for what might make me feel at home.

"Have you ever heard of baking with spent grains?" my coworker Lira asked while shaping buns one day. "I'm kind of curious about it."

In the first phase of beer making, a brewer soaks grains—typically wheat or barley—to extract their sugars, creating the liquid that gets fermented into beer. The resulting grains, stripped of their sweetness, are composted, used as animal feed, or thrown away. But the remaining fiber and protein still contain a great deal of flavor, opening a world of possibilities for the creative baker.

"I've never done it, but I'm curious!" I responded. "Let's give it a try."

Sofra's commitment to teaching attracted bakers brimming with curiosity. We'd watched several bakery alums go on to open their own businesses with Sofra's support. The café stocked spice blends from one alum who had opened a spice shop down the road and macarons from another who was running a wholesale macaron operation. They commissioned paintings from a baker who built a business painting food art. It was common for us to experiment in one another's home kitchens in our off hours.

That afternoon, when our shift ended, Lira and I drove to a local brewery and asked if we could have some of their leftover grains.

"We're going to make bread with it," we told the brewers.

"Well, we don't use it for anything," the owner said. "So I don't see why we can't share."

Over the next few weeks, Lira and I tested all kinds of loaves. We mixed the wet grains into bread dough, dehydrated the grains, and ground them into flour. We used the mash as the base of a sourdough starter, and we researched how to bake with brewer's yeast, looking for ways to match the flavor profile of a bread to the beer it came from.

While stuffing our mouths with a braided creation topped with demerara sugar, Lira asked if we could take our collaboration a step further: "I think we should create a business plan," she said.

We pulled our final batch from the oven and drove to Porter Square Books, where we sat down in the business aisle. After skimming through the titles on the shelves, we selected two books that looked helpful—one a beginner's guide to small business and the other about selling food.

"I think we need to go with a CSA model," I said to Lira after we'd spent a few days researching. Community-supported agriculture (CSA) is a business model popular among small farms. Customers purchase a share of the farm at the beginning of the season, which covers the farmer's expenses up front, and then they receive a box of produce each week for the length of their share. "A CSB—community-supported bread."

"Are you sure you can do all this along with school?" Lira probed.

In between Sofra shifts, graduate classes, meetings with commercial kitchens, and emails to farmers market managers, I was developing a research plan for my master's thesis. I was studying church meals and writing about a theological approach to food. I'd connected with Simple Church, a new church plant an hour west of Boston, which held services around the dinner table. A "dinner church," they called themselves.

I planned to study the Simple Church community for my final graduate project, focusing on how the table builds community and what it can teach us about the value of Communion. I wasn't sure where these ideas would take me, but more possibilities kept coming into view for my future: going to seminary, doing doctoral work, writing for magazines and online publications, opening a future bakery.

I felt as though I were in a dark room pressing against every inch of the walls in search of a door to go through. I was trying to feel my way forward, toward whatever "forward" was supposed to be.

Then, just as I assured Lira I could do it all, my former chef called.

"I'm opening a Greek restaurant," he said. Soon after we'd returned from New York, he'd shared with me his plan to open a place of his own.

"Call me when you're ready," I'd told him the day I started at Sofra. But the longer I'd been out of the restaurant business, the more I wanted to stay out of it. Bakeries—especially those steered by collaborative women—were more my speed.

"I want a simple pastry menu and really good bread. Pita and a crusty sourdough," he said. Those were the right words to make me overlook all the reasons to stay away.

"You won't believe it!" I said as soon as Lira climbed into my car.

We'd arranged to take the same morning off so we could drive to the restaurant supply store to price out ingredients and equipment. "My old chef called—he wants me to help him start his new place!"

"Oh . . . that's great," she responded. "But, um, what does that mean for the bread business?"

"Oh, I'll figure it out," I said quickly. "Don't worry."

Lira sighed.

We rode to the supply store in silence. I was mulling over Chef's offer, lured by the potential for press. I pictured how good my name would look at the bottom of the menu. I thought about the chance of going to the James Beard House again, or maybe winning a James Beard award of my own.

As Lira and I strolled the aisles, taking down prices for the equipment we'd need, my mind was already on the next project.

"Want to grab lunch?" I asked after we wrapped up.

"No, I should get home," Lira responded, aware my attention had already turned.

I dropped her off at her apartment, where she said a solemn goodbye. Before I even drove away, I pulled out my phone.

"I'm in," I texted Chef. "When do we begin?"

11

ON RESILIENCE

Sanctify us also that we may . . . serve you in unity, constancy, and peace.

THE BOOK OF COMMON PRAYER,
"THE HOLY EUCHARIST"

Throughout Scripture, yeast is used to symbolize the spread of the Kingdom of God as well as the power of sin and false teaching. "The kingdom of heaven is like yeast," Jesus says in Matthew 13:33. He goes on to describe a woman mixing yeast into flour until all of it is leavened. Just a few chapters later, though, Jesus uses the image of yeast as a warning: "Be on guard against the yeast of the Pharisees and Sadducees," he cautions in Matthew 16:6, pointing to the leaders whose commitment to religious teaching and practice blinded them from God in their midst.[1]

The environment most conducive to fermenting bread is also the environment most conducive to breeding harmful bacteria. Pathogenic microbes rot food, while beneficial ones provide leavening and flavor. A yeast culture maintains a healthy balance of yeast and bacteria through a symbiotic relationship between the two. The beneficial microbes over-power any damage the pathogenic microbes might do.

To keep a starter healthy, it must be fed daily with flour and water. As the starter breaks down the starches present in the food, it rises and falls. The starter needs to flow through its full cycle to maintain the proper balance between acid and bacteria: rising, resting, and falling every day. If the starter is underfed, especially over a prolonged period of time, the balance of microbes is thrown off. The resulting starter is so pungent it stings the nose and eventually dies.

Rising, falling, resting. This same rhythm practiced in our own lives can build resilience against pathogenic habits that might overpower us, too.

I didn't grow up with icons around. It's possible I learned about them in some of my art history readings during my homeschooling years, but I have no recollection of seeing them until I moved to Boston.

Our apartment was situated between an Eastern Orthodox church and a Catholic parish. Half of our neighbors were students and young professionals, and the other half were older couples who had lived in their homes since the neighborhood had a predominantly Catholic popula-tion. A handful of these older neighbors hung icons at their front doors, which they would touch or kiss every time they stepped inside their homes.

In Christian tradition, iconography is a form of artwork intended to guide a person's devotion to God. The philosophy behind the practice is that an image of Jesus, who is himself the image of the invisible God, facilitates worship by cultivating a desire for God.

Though some critics mistakenly assume that the icon itself is the object of veneration, the focus of such worship is not the object but the God whom the object portrays. Theologian Willie Jennings writes that icons are intended to destroy the worldly desires that keep us from God by "tear-ing open the body's desire and returning it to communion with God."[2]

Because Jesus also exists with us in the form of bread, torn open and offered for our consumption in the Eucharist, I like to think that icons have something to teach us about baking and eating, too.

———————

In the fall of 2015, I took a trip to Montreal with Lyndsey, a friend from my ship days. I drove north through Vermont in its most stunning season, the vibrant oranges and yellows of the trees inviting me to slow down and enjoy. For two days, we wandered up and down the hilly streets of Montreal, visiting chocolate shops and cafés and the historic Jean-Talon Market, cobbling together the little French we'd retained from our time in Benin as we navigated the city.

On Sunday we went to mass at the basilica in Old Montreal, relying on our familiarity with the rhythms of a liturgical service to fill in the gaps where our French language skills failed. When it came time for Communion, Lyndsey and I debated about what to do.

In Catholicism, the Eucharist is reserved for those who are part of the Catholic church and who hold to the church's teachings about the real presence of Christ in the sacrament. As Anglicans, we knew we were supposed to refrain, but given the number of tourists present, we figured we could get away with it. We decided, with a touch of hesitation, to join in.

When we were released from our row, we stood before the priest, hands out and faces still. Lyndsey received her bread and returned to the pew. I crossed myself and then extended my palms.

The priest froze, eyes fixed on something behind me, as though he saw a vision.

He knows, I thought. *God is telling him I shouldn't be here. I'm not supposed to receive this bread.*

I considered running back to my seat, hiding in the crowd of churchgoers to kneel and confess my disrespect for the orders of this congregation. But I stayed, hungry for the wafer in his hands.

After a long pause, the priest broke away from the line of penitents and walked straight to Lyndsey, who was sitting in our pew, head bowed in prayer and wafer still in hand.

"*Mange!*" he told her. "Eat!" He watched her lift the host to her lips, his own face drained of color. Then he returned solemnly to the line and pressed a wafer into my palm.

Despite the awkwardness I felt, I was moved by the concern the priest showed for every piece of Christ's Body distributed in the church. In a building filled with intricate mosaics, stained glass, towering arches, and an organ that stretched the width of the structure, the priest could not look away from the Bread. Like the shepherd who left the ninety-nine to care for the one, he could not divert his attention until he knew each piece was consumed.

He understood it as his role to extend the literal Christ to everyone present, and though he could not confirm that every recipient was worthy to consume, he at least was careful not to let a crumb leave his care.

I wanted to hold such clarity about God's presence in the Bread that I couldn't look away, even amid the beauty all around me. I wanted to bake and eat my own bread with this kind of reverence—a hospitality that views every crumb as worthy of care.

At the time, I was months deep in recipe testing for Chef's new Greek restaurant venture. We'd been offered a six-month pop-up inside a speakeasy-style bar. Wink & Nod called its kitchen a "culinary incubator," and it offered rising chefs six-month trial periods to introduce the city to their concept while they secured funding to build a brick and mortar. Our trial period was set to begin just after the new year, but we were testing the menu through one-off events at various restaurants around town.

After the service, I dropped Lyndsey off at the airport and then drove the five hours back to Boston. When I got home, I mixed up four loaves of sprouted-wheat sourdough for an event the restaurant was hosting the next day. I set my alarm at half-hour increments to stretch and fold the dough through the night, the rhythm of broken sleep its own kind of devotion. As my hands worked the dough, my mind kept returning to thoughts of the worried priest.

The line between an icon and an idol is thin. When the focus remains on God, the icon draws the worshiper into the relational love of God. However, when the focus turns inward, toward something created as an end in itself, rather than as a means of knowing God, an idol is born.

This is true of hospitality as well. When our feasting together points to God, it turns our eyes heavenward. But when hospitality becomes an idol, it is distorted, turning us away from one another and away from God, destroying relationships rather than building them.

The red flags became apparent a few days after my trip to Montreal. I'd been working on the restaurant project for six months without pay, taking extra graduate classes so I could have a lighter semester once our pop-up at Wink & Nod opened. I tested the recipes dozens of times in my home kitchen, using my own savings to purchase ingredients—which Chef promised to reimburse one day.

But the recipes that had worked in my home kitchen hadn't translated well to the commercial kitchen at our recent event. With the exception of the bread, which I'd attended to all through the night, every component flopped: the rose hip meringue fell flat, the pistachio baklava didn't crisp, the semolina halvah crumbled. I was angry at myself, and I was angry at the hosts, who were angry at me. I pushed through the night, promising myself I wouldn't make the same mistakes again. I tested the recipes a few more times before asking Chef about pay, sure that my proven devotion would earn me a livable wage.

He handed me cash to cover my recipe testing and told me my rate to begin in the new year: hardly enough to cover rent.

"Don't go any further," a colleague at school warned. "You can back out now."

My dad agreed. "It already sounds like bad news."

But the publicity had begun, and I was sucked in by the pride of knowing that local food writers were familiar with my name. I hoped that by the end of the pop-up, which fell at the same time as my graduation, I would have secured a dream position: the pastry chef at the newest brick and mortar on Boston's restaurant scene. I took on a side job managing my graduate program's blog and social media and agreed to see the rest of the commitment through.

Two months later, we were moving into the kitchen at Wink & Nod, the narrow driveway behind the restaurant blanketed with a fresh layer of New Year's snow. We had forty-eight hours to rearrange the equipment to our liking and prep the ingredients for opening night—I worked about thirty out of those forty-eight hours. Not uncommon for the restaurant industry, but exhausting nonetheless.

To help us manage the workload, Wink & Nod supplied us with a few of their cooks, who were even more crass than the ones I'd worked with in the restaurant two years before. They'd plate up staff meals in phallic shapes and laugh as they watched others eat, while the managers joked about which guests at the bar they planned to bed. One food runner told me that women are too shrill when they're in charge, and he could never let a woman tell him what to do. So though I was his superior, my title offered no authority. Another cook retorted that our whole team was out of sync because I refused to bond with them at the bar after work.

"Just this once?" he asked every night, offering me a blunt. "I'll buy your beers."

The anger in the kitchen amplified my anxiety. Cooks slammed pots all day long and growled at coworkers who were in their way. Chef shouted and kicked the coolers when the ticket machine got out of control. I was surprised by my own short temper in response. Yet thanks to my gender, I was the only cook who got scolded for my tone.

"Can you just keep your head down and ignore it all?" my therapist asked me.

I'd begun seeing him after accepting the job, in the midst of juggling recipe testing, an increased class load, and stress over my impending graduation. Though I couldn't name the source of my worry, I was anxious about next steps. My studies hadn't clarified a career path for me aside from more restaurant work, which, mingled with a heavy dose of vanity, was the reason I'd accepted this position. I hoped it would lead to a long-term role.

Like my father and my friends, my therapist's first recommendation was that I quit. But when it became apparent that I wouldn't listen, he began suggesting alternative means of dealing with the stress. "Maybe you could pray while you bake?"

At the prompting of my therapist, I began reciting Saint Patrick's Breastplate every day as I shaped pita, each phrase matching the movements of my hands: *Christ behind me, Christ before me, Christ beside me. Christ in the mouth of everyone who speaks of me.*

I willed Christ to shield me from the environment I was in, to permeate the food I sent out to others. But as the weeks wore on, I felt less connected to my body and more compelled to shrink back into the recesses of my mind.

My days went something like this:

8:00 Pull myself out of bed.
9:00 Head to a coffee shop to work on an assignment for school or write a piece for my side job.
11:30 Catch a bus to the South End.
11:31 Feel my heart begin to palpitate.
11:41 Breathe deeply enough to slow my heart rate down, then step off the bus and walk into the restaurant.
11:45 Change from my winter coat to my chef's coat and begin daily prep.
1:30 Grow tense as my coworkers begin to arrive.
4:30 Set up my station for service.
5:00 Work the line.

10:00   Clean the kitchen.
11:00   Ride the train back home.
12:00   Shower, then watch a TV show to slow the adrenaline rush.
 1:00   Attempt to sleep.
 8:00   Begin again.

I passed my church every day on my commute. Despite the physical proximity between work and my place of worship, the chasm between the two was deep. Singing alongside the congregation on Sunday felt strange after the words slung at me every night during the week.

"Kendall, I haven't seen you in a while," my priest said when I ran into him at a coffee shop before work one day.

"Yeah. I just started a new job," I told him, "The kitchen's right down the street from here."

"I saw you're not on hospitality rotation anymore," he responded. "I would love to help you get more involved!"

Though I tried, I couldn't adequately convey the stress of my job. Our church was full of academics and businesspeople, lawyers and campus ministers. I struggled to fit the rigors of shift work and manual labor with the rhythms of church life, so I stopped trying to make it work. I figured I'd return once the pop-up was done, but for now, the extra sleep felt like a better means of practicing Sabbath.

By mid-February, I was worn thin. I pulled Chef aside and told him I couldn't keep working in these conditions.

"Rein in the crew, or I'm out," I told him.

"I will, I will," he promised.

Chef didn't tell anyone that the request to cut back on the explicit humor came from me, but he didn't have to—I was the only one who failed to participate. One coworker apologized for making me feel uncomfortable. The rest just gave me glares. They checked their language for a week or two and then returned full force—Chef included.

I stayed.

By March, my roommates began to express their worry.

"Where's the line?" Emily asked one Sunday. We'd taken advantage of the rare warm March day and my even rarer day off, and headed to a rocky beach on Boston's south shore. We laid out on boulders near the water's edge and listened to the waves crash.

"What's enough to make you quit?"

I sighed. "If they call me one of two names," I responded.

She laughed in disbelief when I told her the terms that were deal breakers for me.

"They would never . . ." she said. "Would they?"

The next morning, I began to panic on the platform at Harvard Square station as my train pulled in. I blinked back tears and slowed my breathing, willing myself to step on board.

"It happened," I texted Emily the following Saturday as I rode the train home. "I was called a c— and a w—." I couldn't even bear to type the full words.

When I opened the door to the apartment, Emily and her boyfriend stood waiting. They wrapped me in their arms as I sobbed.

"So, did you quit?" Emily asked when my crying slowed.

"No," I said. "I can't."

Within an industry that prides itself on hospitality to guests, there is little hospitality to the women and men who work behind the scenes. But the challenge of that cook three years before rang in my ears—I had to learn to endure the harassment if I wanted a career in this field.

Only I wasn't so sure I did.

My parents, concerned for my well-being, invited me to join them and my older sister at the beach over Palm Sunday weekend. My dad went every spring for a work trip, and he wanted Alyssa and me to come along this year. At first I declined. I'd committed to the pop-up knowing it would demand my full attention for a while. I didn't want anyone to question my dedication, especially when they already had something against me. I couldn't give any more fodder by asking for a weekend away. But by the middle of March, I was desperate to escape. I put in my request for time off.

For three days I sat on the beach with a Marilynne Robinson novel in hand and a book of poetry in my bag. I never opened either of the books, though. I just stared out at the ocean, thinking about what I was missing out on by working this job and the longings I was masking through overworking.

I hadn't gone on a date in months. When I was engrossed in work, I could convince myself I preferred being single. I could shove down the memory of the date who had eyed my body up and down then refused to look at me while we talked, disappointed by all the curves he saw. I could ignore that the man I'd been interested in was now dating a close friend and that a different friend I'd confessed my feelings to didn't return my affections. Another guy, someone I'd been set up with on a blind date, told the matchmaker he couldn't go out with a woman who exceeded him in academic drive—he canceled before we'd ever met.

The sun scorched my shoulders as I listened to the waves. The thoughts about myself washed up until I couldn't dam them back anymore. I was too much: too fat, too loud, too educated, too intense for the life I'd thought I wanted—a quiet life of marriage and children and building community around bread.

And I was not enough: not tough enough, not crass enough, not man enough for the life I was in.

When I tried to stand my ground at work, I was too much there, too: too shrill, too petty, too weak. I refused to let the kitchen staff feel like they'd broken me, so despite the mountain of reasons to quit, I stayed.

On Monday I returned to work, my heart racing once again as I transferred from the train to the bus. It was Holy Week, but I wasn't ready to journey to Easter with my church. Head down, I prayed silently as I shaped another hundred pita. I drowned out the jeers of my coworkers and held back my tears, marking my own Holy Week of sorts. I wished

I were back on an island in the middle of the Caribbean Sea, the water buffering me from the cruel laughter all around.

On Tuesday and Wednesday I walked the three and a half miles to the kitchen. Unlike the bus route, which drove me straight to the alley behind the restaurant, I could divert my steps at any moment. I could choose to walk somewhere else instead. I wouldn't, but I could.

On Thursday I couldn't stop thinking about this ironic kind of hospitality. I wondered if the cooks behind Jesus' last meal were as difficult as the ones who cooked with me.

On Good Friday and Holy Saturday, I worked some more.

I can't remember if I went to church on Easter or if I slept in. I can't remember if the restaurant offered brunch. I suppose it's fitting that the day is a blur. I wasn't ready for resurrection.

I continued this daily rhythm for two more weeks until my friend Heather, another baker, took me to coffee. We drove to Concord, home of Louisa May Alcott and Henry David Thoreau. Clouds gathered overhead as we rolled away from the city. I told her about the culture of the kitchen, about my anxiety attacks on my way into work. I brushed it off as normal—in the restaurant industry, it so often is. She listened to me, nodding, while we walked into the café, just in time to avoid the clouds bursting open.

"You can decide to be done today," she told me, holding her mug of chai as rain pattered against the window.

"It's just a few more months," I countered, sipping my third coffee of the day. "I can do anything for a few months."

"You never have to walk through that door again."

I didn't have the will to object anymore. I wanted to cry, to burst open like the clouds overhead, but I had nothing left to give.

Stepping away meant leaving behind a dream, even if it was a dream I no longer wanted. I knew that quitting this job meant quitting this industry. While I could find another kitchen to hire me, I wouldn't have the will to step inside another restaurant kitchen again.

Heather and I talked through the fears that had kept me from leaving. Greatest among them was a resistance to being known as someone who quits. I would let the industry break me before I would let it take my pride. Unable to feel anymore, I admitted the restaurant had won. I was broken.

I climbed back into my car to call my mom. As I drove through the rain, I told her I would need financial help until I figured out what to do. I'd used up all my savings preparing for the pop-up, and I could barely make ends meet on my current salary.

"You need out," she replied. "We'll help you."

Armed with the support of family and friends, I went to work the next day and pulled Chef aside.

"I can't do this anymore," I told him. "Tomorrow's my last day. Don't tell anyone until I'm gone."

I prepared enough dessert and bread to get them through the next few days while he scrambled to figure out a replacement. Then I packed up my knife kit and walked away, the rhythm mirroring the day I'd packed up my pointe shoes for the last time.

I didn't know what to do with myself after I left. I walked to the dance studio in Cambridge Square and signed up for adult ballet classes. It had been years since I'd worn a leotard or canvas shoes, but I needed to use my body in a way that brought me joy.

The studio floors squeaked with each tendu, the pianist's music filling the space around us. I couldn't move as smoothly as I had in high school or college, but as sweat dripped down my back and my arms burned, extended into second position, I returned to my body once again.

Every morning I fed my sourdough starter, adjusting the volume and temperature of the feedings to accommodate the shifts in the weather. Sourdough begs for slow rhythms, for tender observation to stay alive. The yeasts cause the starter to bubble and swell, then to fall again, a cycle it must flow through each day in order to balance the microbial makeup of the culture. I watched its rhythmic breathing, marveling at the way it transformed the flour I mixed in.

The artist who crafts icons is called an icon writer, pointing the attention away from her skill as an artist and toward her task of making the Word visible. The craft of icon writing is its own form of worship, turning the writer's attention toward God with each layer of paint—not unlike the ways our attention is shaped through contemplation of the finished piece.

As I mixed up my sourdough each day, I prayed that like the icon writer, God might allow this bread to direct my attention and, in so doing, heal me.

12

ON HOME

The Body of Christ, the bread of heaven.

THE BOOK OF COMMON PRAYER,
"THE HOLY EUCHARIST"

SOMERVILLE, MASSACHUSETTS

According to some bakers, yeast is influenced by its geographic location. They swear that yeast flavors dough with the taste of a particular place—that the culture carries the unique strains of the city where it was first brought to life. Amateur and professional bakers alike are won over by the romantic idea of a centuries-old starter, maintained for generations and moved around the world, connecting bakers across location and time.

Other bakers claim that the culture changes wherever the starter goes. As a sourdough starter swells and grows and falls again, the colony of yeasts and bacteria repopulate to match the strains around them. A sourdough starter built in France two hundred years ago and then fed and fostered for a while in my home, they say, won't be any different from the one I mixed up a few weeks ago myself.

Scientists who study the microbiome of bread aren't sure what role location plays. Like the porous boundaries between body and bread, there is undoubtedly some kind of connection; they just don't know exactly how the imprinting happens.

I like to imagine that yeast creates a home wherever it lands. It brings a taste of the place it comes from but grows and changes with its local community too.

"Welcome, welcome, welcome to Simple Church!" Pastor Zach bellowed in the church fellowship hall, guitar strapped across his chest. The chatter in the room quieted as everyone turned to stand in a circle around six tables draped in red. Twinkle lights hung from the ceiling, supplementing the light that flickered from white candles atop each table. On the far end of the room, a potluck spread of potato soup, arugula salad, mac and cheese, and a chocolate pie sat ready to feed a hungry crowd.

As Zach began to strum, kids scurried to the center of the room to dance. "This little light of mine, I'm gonna let it shine," the congregation sang together. Toddlers jumped and twirled in worship to accompany the song.

"We gather tonight, and every Thursday night, to feast," Zach continued when the song was over and the children had calmed down. "We gather to break bread in memory of another meal that happened on a Thursday night, when Jesus sat with his disciples."

Zach raised a five-pound loaf of bread above his head. As he tore it in half, steam rose from the center. I'd twisted the dough into a braid just hours before.

"Yesterday this bread was flour, water, salt, and yeast. Four different ingredients that are now mixed together. You can't separate them anymore. Just like this bread, we're all different but joined together when we share this loaf."

At Zach's feet, a toddler raised her hands, opening and closing her fists while bouncing from foot to foot. She giggled as Zach leaned over to hand her a piece of bread.

"Christ's Body, broken for you," Zach said. She closed her eyes and savored the bite before running back to her mom.

Soon after I left the restaurant pop-up, Simple Church offered me a job. I'd gotten to know Pastor Zach, the church's founder, while interviewing congregants for my final graduate project. When he planted the church, in a small town an hour west of Boston, he cast a vision for a community that would sustain itself through food.

Some church members volunteered on a local farm in exchange for produce to serve at their Thursday-night service, which took place over the course of a meal. Others baked bread together and then sold it at the local farmers market, sustaining the congregation's financial needs while also allowing them to get to know the folks in town.

Two years in, they were looking for help scaling the bread program. After my grad school project was complete, I continued communicating with them, offering tips and tweaking their recipes. When Zach found out I was looking for a job, he reached out.

"We want to start a weekly bread share," he told me. "Like a CSA, but for bread. Do you think that would work?"

"I think so—I have some business plans for that kind of model already," I responded, rifling through my desk for the ideas Lira and I had brainstormed together.

"Awesome!" he exclaimed. "We're about to start fundraising for a wood-fired oven. Can you help me draw up a plan for the pitch?"

I needed the shift in pace and work mentality that Simple Church offered. I felt myself relax on my commute as the city streets opened up into the Massachusetts countryside. We started our mornings at the parsonage, praying together and eating a breakfast of eggs and coffee while the chickens clucked just outside the window. Then we'd head to the church kitchen, where we shaped and baked loaves in preparation for the market. Church members helped at every stage of the process:

some joined in the shaping and baking, some packaged the loaves, some worked the tent at the market, and some helped clean.

The bread had started as a fundraising opportunity, but by the time I began working at Simple Church, it had grown into much more. The collaborative process enabled those who might not fit into traditional church leadership roles to find a way to engage with their hands. It empowered those who couldn't give financially to support the church with their time. The youth could participate by selling bread at the market. And customers wary of religion felt welcomed into the fold as they returned each week for a fresh loaf.

The Thursday-evening service allowed me to work for the church while maintaining membership at my home church in Boston. Between the two—the formal, liturgical Sunday service and the casual Thursday-evening one—I experienced the full beauty of what the church can be, in all its diversity.

I loved Simple Church and the people who attended. I loved the slow rhythms and the long drive—a stark contrast to the restaurant industry. But by the following spring, nine months into my tenure, my restlessness returned once again.

I dubbed that season the spring of weddings. Four of the women closest to me, including my older sister and my roommate Emily, would be getting married in the span of six weeks, all in different cities. In between the bridal showers and the weddings, my brother announced his engagement, too. I was set to make two wedding cakes, one loaf of Communion bread, and four hundred Earl Grey caramel candy favors, plus write and deliver two maid of honor speeches.

It was a season of joy and celebration, and of loss and loneliness.

"I want what they have," I whispered in prayer on my drive into work, hymns playing softly in the background. "I want a partner. I want a place to call home, where roommates don't just get married and leave."

Sometimes my pleas carried a bit more desperation, born out of the ongoing series of rejections from men I'd been interested in. "What's wrong with me?" I would cry to the Lord. "Why doesn't anyone ever see me or want me?"

Our apartment filled up with wedding accessories: boxes full of silver table chargers, rose-scented votives, hand-painted table numbers. I tried on my bridesmaid dresses and examined the fit in the dining room mirror while Emily checked the adjustments to her gown.

To try and keep costs down for us, she'd chosen a bridesmaid dress on clearance. While I was grateful for the savings, the largest size the company offered was a size too small for me. In the weeks leading up to the wedding, I found myself scrambling for ways to make it fit—extra laps in the pool at the gym, long walks around the neighborhood. I prayed I wouldn't have to resort to any sort of restrictive eating. I worried that even a few days spent dropping water weight would undo all the work of the past few years, learning to see food as a gift from God.

When Emily and her fiancé left one Saturday to look at apartments, I sat on the couch and looked at the wedding paraphernalia all around before scrolling through the growing number of unanswered texts on my phone.

"Kendall, can you call me so we can plan Alyssa's bachelorette party?" one of Alyssa's friends asked.

"Hey Kendall, just wanted to see if you've figured out where you're going to stay yet," texted Hannah, from high school, whose wedding was third in line.

"Can we chat about what kind of bread you'll be making for Communion?" wrote Kayla, whose wedding was the fourth and final one.

"How hard would it be for you to make ice cream for our wedding?" Davis asked, looking ahead to the following spring.

I flipped through the contacts in my phone to find someone who didn't have wedding details on their mind. I was tired of hiding my grief at home and on the phone, allowing only excitement to show in front of these friends. And I *was* excited for them. At the same time, their daily routines were changing, as were their relational needs. While their focus shifted more and more toward their future spouses, my need for them remained the same.

I stared at my contact list, realizing that every person I would call in moments of loneliness was busy making wedding plans of her own. I threw my phone across the living room and went into the bathroom, where I sat in the shower and let the water flow while I sobbed.

"Please, God," I said between tears. "I don't want to be single anymore. I want a partner. I want a family. I want a place to call home."

I turned on my phone just before the plane's wheels hit the tarmac. A red bubble notified me that I'd missed a call and a voicemail.

"Kendall. It's Morgan, from the Duke Divinity admissions office."

On a whim, I'd sent an application for a two-year theology program the November before, when I panicked that Simple Church might not have the budget to pay me for another year. In my application, I proposed a project researching the connection between theology and bread. But I wasn't sure if I was ready to move quite yet, or if I was ready to go back to school. I wanted to ground myself in a community and in a place; I wanted to resist the urge to keep pressing forward—the one that had driven my restlessness in the years before. The Simple Church position incorporated all my interests, and I loved the community. It made sense to stay.

"We'd like to offer you full funding to start this fall," Morgan's message continued.

I sat in my seat, breathing through a flood of emotions: relief, excitement, and a twinge of disappointment as well. It was an offer too good to refuse.

I called my dad as I rolled my suitcase through the airport. "Well, I guess I'm moving to North Carolina," I told him, attempting to override my sadness about leaving Massachusetts and Simple Church behind.

"Congratulations! I'm so proud of you," he said. "Have fun at Alyssa's bridal shower this weekend."

Two months later, between weddings two and three, I went to coffee with an editor looking to acquire a book based on my research at Boston University.

"You've got a lot of books in you," she said as we sipped lattes. "Take your writing seriously."

Within another two months, I'd been offered my first reported feature for *Christianity Today*, a piece about seminaries with food and theology programs.

It was a strange season, this celebration of my friends' nuptials alongside the celebration of an unexpected turn in my career. As grateful as I was for the opportunities, they felt like my plan B. I would have given them all up in exchange for a partner, for children, for a stable job and home.

I longed for someone to tell me I was beautiful, that my body was good. I longed to love and be loved. I longed for someone to embrace me, not reject me, when I shared the way I felt. But as I prayed for stability, for daily bread, it felt like God kept offering me cake instead.

The warnings of a dozen church ladies took up residence in my mind. As a child, I'd heard the murmurs about single women. I wondered what the church ladies would say to me in this moment: "Be careful not to make your career your whole life," they'd warn. "By the time you realize how much you want kids, it might be too late!"

I wanted these fictional ladies whispering in my mind to know that the opposite was true. My budding career felt like a stand-in for my actual desire, like something God had given to tide me over while saying no to my deeper longing.

When I wrote on the topic of singleness, attempting to articulate this pain, readers made comments like "God will give you the desire of your heart once you let go and trust him. You shouldn't want something so bad."

"You're still so young!" my friends told me when I shared with them the weariness of my unmet prayers. "Don't worry—you have plenty of time."

"I'm not worried," I snapped, the pointed ache of undesirability punctuating my response. "I'm just lonely *right now*. I'm not afraid it'll never happen; I'm just telling you how it hurts *today*."

With each bad date, though, I became less and less sure my relationship status would ever change. It felt as though God had plastered a neon sign across my forehead, blinking the words *off limits* to any person I found attractive. I *had* to believe that this prolonged singleness was ordained by God. The only way for me to avoid the spiral of questioning whether I was the problem was to believe that God was strategically withholding a partner from me.

"You said it's not good to be alone," I would pray. In the creation story, after calling plants, animals, skies, and seas good, God halted the refrain with the creation of one man. "It's not good that the human is alone," God says in Genesis 2:18 (CEB), just before making a partner for Adam.

I'd heard the passage cited over and over. "We were made for relationship," a pastor would say, "and in the covenant of marriage, that relational need is filled."

But as I begged the Lord to provide in the area I most desired, God gently but firmly made the answer clear: "No. I'm offering another path instead."

There were no simple answers for these competing emotions, no easy resolution for this tension between celebration and pain. Some days I was able to muster acceptance, even gratitude, for this life I hadn't chosen. But other days, like when friends at each wedding asked why I wasn't seeing anyone, the loneliness was too crushing to bear.

I didn't doubt that God loved me, that God had a purpose for me, that God was present with me. But I couldn't reconcile God's love with God's silence over my deeper plea. Cake, though wonderful, cannot sustain anyone for the long haul.

Rather than fast from any particular item that Lent, I'd committed to writing about sourdough three times a week. In this season of both celebration and loss, I couldn't handle giving up anything more. I asked God to fill me through the bread instead as I probed what the wild yeasts had to teach: about God, about death, about the hope of resurrection, about the flavor of a particular place.

For six weeks I sat down at a coffee shop or in the library every Monday, Wednesday, and Friday to write a theological reflection. On the days in between, I baked.

As I watched my sourdough starter bubble and burp, I contemplated both the beauty and the sadness of the fact that yeasts repopulate when they arrive in a new place. Within a few feedings in my North Carolina home, I wondered, would there be anything distinctive about the starter to suggest its place of origin? Would it be as confused as I was about what city it was from? Or would it teach me to make a home wherever I might land?

I carried this tension of wanting to be grounded but also wanting to move as I prepared to say goodbye. I wept over leaving the very people who had taught me to value my connection to place, the very churches that had taught me to crave simplicity. While these communities had helped me value the things that made me want to stay, they also shaped my wonder for bread—the reason I needed to go.

During the Easter vigil, I joined three other dancers for a piece choreographed to the story of the valley of dry bones.[1]

"Prophesy over these bones," God tells the prophet Ezekiel as he stands in the dry valley, overlooking hundreds of bones.

The rhythmic tone of the reading builds: "Prophesy!" God says. The bones rattle and then come together, bone to bone, until they are cloaked in sinews and flesh.

"Prophesy to the breath!" God says again, further building the momentum. Then, mirroring the Creation account in Genesis, the bodies fill with life, animated by the breath of God.

At the end of the reading, while the music team played a rendition of a song called "Dry Bones," the four of us slipped out of the pews and began dancing down the center aisle of the church.

As the music came to a crescendo, we worked our way toward the front, like the sinews and skin in the passage that slowly drew together. The growing energy of the song, and of our dance, paralleled the building energy of the passage.

At the time the book of Ezekiel was written, Israel was in exile in Babylon. They felt abandoned by God, torn from the land God had promised them, worried they would lose their distinctive cultural and religious identity. This longing for community—for stability and home—is part of the way God created us as humans.

We were made to be in relationship with others, and we were made to be rooted and grounded in God's creation. Throughout Scripture, the relationship between a people and their place is emphasized again and again, as is God's promise to be with God's people when they venture on their own way. In this passage about dry bones, God promises to restore the Israelites to their soil, to their home. It validates the desire to be grounded in a place, as well as God's presence in our wandering.

I felt this tension, this longing for a settled home, every time we rehearsed the piece in the weeks before the vigil. Having lived in so many places over the course of my life—four different states plus three more countries while docked on a boat—I was ready to root myself somewhere.

Boston, my roommates, and my second-floor apartment had all shaped me as I ventured into adulthood. They imprinted my work and my understanding of vocation. The hospitality shared within the walls of that apartment sparked direction and brought healing in the midst of hard times.

But without Emily, the home no longer held the same pull. As much as I wanted to keep dancing at this vigil every year, to keep sharing bread with both my Sunday-morning church and my Thursday-night community, I knew I was being called away.

In truth, as much as I wanted to stay, I also wanted to go.

The next morning, Easter Sunday, I was stationed in the back right corner of the sanctuary during Communion to offer prayer for anyone who came requesting intercession. My friend Bethany came walking toward me, her eyes red.

"I got my period . . . again," she said before bursting into tears.

We hugged and cried. I prayed over her through tears as babies babbled in the laps of their parents a few pews over, their hair still dripping from the baptism ceremony minutes before. Bethany and her husband had been trying for a second child for years, but the tangible reminder of unanswered prayer arrived each month, like clockwork.

Four weeks later, on Mother's Day, our eyes met across the sanctuary. She sighed and looked down before turning back to her conversation with the music team. She didn't need to say anything more. Along both sides of the sanctuary, every window was propped open to let in the light Boston breeze and the chirps of black-capped chickadees. The birds accompanied every song Bethany led that morning. I prayed for her and her family through each one.

At the end of the service, as I walked to the front of the church to receive Communion, I felt as though God had turned the verse from Genesis back toward me. I looked at the people around me, all sharing from the same loaf and the same cup. In this meal, we committed ourselves to one another as Christ's own body. We took on one another's sorrow as well as one another's joy.

In this meal, God seemed to whisper to me, *I provide for the lonely.* This meal was a covenant before God of bread and wine, forming us together into a new family. Those who were single, married, infertile, struggling through sleepless newborn days, full of youth, or nearing the end of their time on earth all recognized together that no one could say to the other, "I do not need you."

I needed them: their prayers, their hugs, and their handshakes. Their dinner tables bustling with chatty children. I needed their friendship, their conversation, their words of affirmation, and their love.

And they needed me: my presence, my flexibility, my willingness to listen to the same child's joke told for the thousandth time.

It was this mutual need that made the goodbye so hard, but it recast my understanding of God's presence in my loneliness too.

Through these goodbyes, I had to release my own plan once again, exchanging my vision of a slow, simple life for the life God was offering me instead. Like Ezekiel, I had to trust that my desire for family, my desire to be rooted in a particular place was good. And I had to release my vision for how that might come to be.

As I prepared to move, I determined to create in Durham a home that would foster a sense of family through hospitality. Perhaps, I hoped, by welcoming others into my home, the edges of my loneliness would dull. Or perhaps the sense of family, even if it wasn't a biological one, would satiate me.

SPELT PITA

If anything made the dark months devoted to the restaurant pop-up worth it, it was the recipes I developed along the way. This pita relies on a technique called a prefermentation: a short fermentation of the whole-grain flour before the rest of the ingredients are mixed in. This step softens the fibrous parts of the grain, pulling out more flavor and creating a tender texture in the dough.

1 cup spelt flour
2 tablespoons honey
1 tablespoon instant yeast
1 cup room-temperature water

¼ cup olive oil
2 cups all-purpose flour
1 teaspoon kosher salt

1. Combine the spelt flour, honey, instant yeast, and water in a mixing bowl. Let the mixture sit for 20 minutes until small bubbles begin to appear on the surface.
2. Add the olive oil, all-purpose flour, and kosher salt. Stir together just until a shaggy dough begins to form (it should be cohesive but a little lumpy). Let rest for 15 minutes.
3. Turn the dough onto the counter and knead for 10 minutes. Using the heel of your hand, push down firmly, then rotate 90 degrees. Fold in half, and repeat. Continue this process for 10–12 minutes, or until the dough is smooth.
4. Once your dough has come together in a smooth ball, place in a well-oiled bowl, cover loosely with a damp tea towel or plastic wrap, and let rest for an hour.
5. Divide your dough into 10 even pieces. Shape each piece into a ball by cupping your hands and rotating between your palms. Once shaped, let the rounds rest another hour while preheating the oven to 400°F.
6. Place an empty baking sheet in the oven. Using a rolling pin, roll the dough one piece at a time into 6-inch circles. Let rest for 5 minutes.
7. Quickly place dough circles onto the hot baking sheet and return to the oven. Bake for 4 minutes. Be careful when you remove your pita from the oven—the bread will puff with steam while baking, which can burn you if the pita deflates while you remove it.

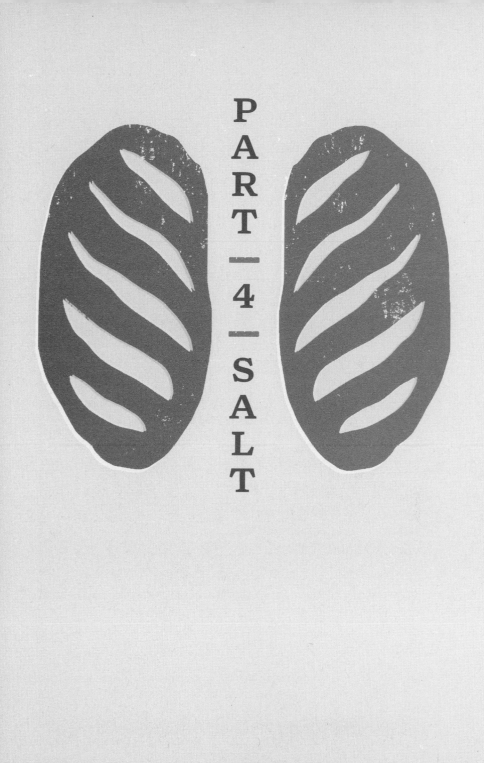

PART 4 SALT

Often thought ancillary,
salt brings rest—
slowing yeast
to a livable pace.

Salt brings color,
opens taste buds to flavor,
and builds gluten strength.

Bread without salt
might still be bread
but not the sort that sings
of life.

13

ON HOSPITALITY

Grant us strength and courage to love and serve you
with gladness and singleness of heart.

THE BOOK OF COMMON PRAYER,
"THE HOLY EUCHARIST"

DURHAM, NORTH CAROLINA

Throughout the Old Testament, salt is often used as a means of making a covenant with God: Leviticus, Numbers, and 2 Chronicles all speak of a covenant of salt. Some scholars speculate that the preservative qualities of salt were intended to remind people of the enduring nature of a covenant with God, a covenant that would carry on from generation to generation.[1] Salt was a sign not just of God's enduring commitment to people but also of the people's enduring commitment to God. "You shall not omit from your grain-offerings the salt of the covenant with your God; with all your offerings you shall offer salt," the Lord said to Moses in Leviticus 2:13 (NRSV).

German theologian Hermann Eising writes that the covenant of salt brings a notion of hospitality to the covenant between the Israelites and God. The salt turns simple elements of grain and meat into a proper meal, making God's intimate promises known through the table.[2] This understanding of a covenant with God being made known through a meal foreshadows the bread and wine offered to us as Christ's own Body and Blood, a meal shared with God and with God's people as a promise of ongoing presence and healing.

It is through these elements, this food and drink, that we know God is with us. Every time we gather to feast with family and friends, we remember God's promises. And in the times we are unable to feast with others, we can trust that—at the very least—God is present, feasting with us when we're on our own.

———

"Can you shop for a dining table?" I asked a college friend who lived in North Carolina, an hour west of Durham. I was still in Massachusetts, scouring apartment listings for my move in early August, and she'd volunteered to help me find secondhand furniture for the new place. "I want something big enough to host dinner parties . . . so seating for about ten?"

The process of searching for and dreaming about where I could live allowed me to imagine what it would feel like to spread out and set down roots. I craved a refuge from school where I could bake and write in a space all my own. And I wanted a place that could host the community of friends I hoped to make.

After weeks of searching, I found the perfect spot: a sunny duplex in Old West Durham, just over a mile from the divinity school. The bathroom, built inside a former closet, was so small that I had to keep the door open if I wanted to move around, and the kitchen cabinets didn't stay shut without the help of baby locks. But the living room had enough space to hold a large table, and the kitchen was big enough to cook with friends. I secured the house, sight unseen, a few weeks before I was due to arrive in town.

I studied the photos and measurements sent by the rental company and then forwarded them to my friend. Estimating the average size of windows and doorframes, we drew up designs and found furniture to fit the specifications.

"Is three feet by six feet too big?" she messaged me one day. "Because I found a hundred-year-old table that looks really cool. The seller's grandfather made it by hand."

"Will you even have room for a couch?" my mom asked when I told her about my furniture plan. "Besides, you don't even know ten people there."

"But I will," I argued. "And I want to be able to have them for dinner when I do."

———

"Hi, I'm Brett," said the tall blond man sitting next to me at orientation. He smiled as we shook hands and struck up a conversation about our research interests—his focus on poetry and mine on bread.

"My wife, Haley, and I moved here from Richmond," he said. "I've been teaching high school the past few years."

As we wandered from one orientation meeting to the next, we talked about the communities we'd left behind to begin school in Durham. While we both had some acquaintances in the area and good friends in nearby towns, neither of us knew anyone in our program yet.

Out of the corner of my eye, I saw a man with a brown beard thumbing the pages of his schedule. He fit the profile I'd been told to look for.

"Oh, I think I need to say hello to that person," I told Brett as we stood near the snack table between meetings. Balancing a cup of coffee and a cookie in one hand, along with my orientation packet, I made my way through the crowd.

"Hey, Micah?" I asked after making eye contact. "I'm Kendall—I went to Wheaton. I think we have some mutual friends?"

"Oh, yeah!" he responded. "I hear you're the person who might be able to answer some questions about bread."

"That's me." I chuckled in response.

Micah joined Brett and me at the next meeting, where they discussed a shared love of the twentieth-century French mystic Simone Weil.

"Would y'all want to meet up at the farmers market on Saturday morning?" Brett asked after our final orientation session. "There's a great spot for biscuits and coffee. And Haley would love to meet you."

Our farmers market breakfast led to a series of midweek dinner parties, where we rotated from house to house, each serving our own homemade loaves. We'd meet in Brett's living room for a potluck lunch after church on Sundays and around my table for a pot of soup on Wednesdays. I couldn't afford ten dining chairs, which I discovered would each cost about as much as the table itself. Instead, I opted for a long bench on each side.

A few days after I moved into the apartment, I found two coral-colored chairs by my neighbor's driveway, waiting for trash pickup day. I dragged them to my house and set one at each end of the table. The benches and chairs squeaked under the slightest bit of weight, and the flat wooden seats were uncomfortable for any extended amount of time. I didn't care, though. I had a home for hosting that was all mine.

From time to time, we'd close our evening by pulling out a Bible and *The Book of Common Prayer*, lighting candles and praying together using the Compline liturgy.

The first time we prayed those words together, I thought back to the women I'd gathered with each week in Boston to do the same. Before my move, they'd prayed for me to find friends I could share Compline with in my new home. There was a sweetness to these new friendships, born out of our common pursuit of a theological degree.

Still, my loneliness persisted.

The fullness I felt as we hugged goodbye after dinner turned to grief as soon as I was alone in my empty apartment.

"I haven't really met any women," I told Margarita on the phone one night. "I mean, these guys are great, and so is Haley. But it would be nice to have a female friend at school. Especially someone who's single."

"I'll pray for that," she responded. "How is Micah?"

"He's great—I can't believe we didn't hang out at Wheaton."

"Uh-huh," she added, probing for more.

"It hurts too much to hope for anything," I responded.

The next day in class, a woman named Claire sat beside me. She'd moved to Durham from the Pacific Northwest, where she'd worked in a charismatic prison ministry. Like me, she'd found healing in the liturgical practices of the Anglican Communion after being in a church community that preyed on her anxiety.

"This might sound weird, but . . . can we be friends?" she asked. "I haven't really made friends with any other women in our program. But you seem cool!"

I laughed, struck by the timing after Margarita's prayer. "I'd love that," I said.

A few weeks after moving to Durham, I sat in a red, cushioned seat in the cinder block sanctuary of St. Titus' Episcopal Church. I was already tired of looking for a new church home. Between the sadness of leaving my community in Boston and the overwhelm of meeting so many new colleagues at school, I hardly had the energy to navigate a new church, especially on my own.

When I sat down at St. Titus, Durham's historically Black Episcopal church, I heard the words and prayers of the liturgy that had carried me from Tanzania to Wheaton to Boston and now here, and I sighed in relief.

I looked at the bulletin in my hands and saw what was written across the cover: "Welcome home."

St. Titus was started in the 1880s by Ms. A. L. Ledger, a Black member of a white Episcopal church who wanted to share the Anglican tradition with her community. While her status and education afforded her full communion in the white church, she longed to share the liturgy with those who didn't possess her freedom to assimilate. By gathering a community to worship in homes and Black-owned businesses around town, she bridged her love of both Episcopal rhythms and Black church tradition. For more than a century, St. Titus had been shaping the city of Durham: organizing for civil rights, advocating on behalf of refugees, reaching out to those with AIDS, and mentoring college students at the campus across the street.

In contrast to the churches I'd been part of before, there were few other members my age. The community held the wisdom of men and women who'd been members of the church through many phases of life—people who had been married, raised their children, and baptized their grandchildren in this place. The narthex displayed the church's respect for the generations who had come before, with news clippings and artwork honoring the historic figures who had helped shape both the city and the church community.

"The peace of Christ be with you," Ms. Vivienne said, gripping my hand and looking into my eyes. She lingered several seconds after I responded, "And also with you." Then she repeated the rhythm with everyone else in the sanctuary while others came to greet me in a similar manner. The passing of the peace lasted at least ten minutes, long enough for us all to meander through the aisles and greet one another by name.

After finding our way back to our seats, we transitioned to the Eucharist liturgy. As the pianist began to play the melody for the Lord's Prayer, Mrs. Adorker took my right hand and Mr. Murphy reached over the seats to grab my left. We held hands as we sang the prayer, raising our arms for the final line: "For thine is the kingdom, and the power, and the glory, forever and ever amen." It didn't matter that I had terrible pitch; most others in the church did too.

I returned to the church each Sunday, drawn in by the hand-holding, the off-key singing, the stories shared with me over chicken biscuits and sweet tea—and that line plastered across the bulletin: *Welcome Home*.

I realized that the church would serve a different role in my life than church had served before. It would not be the center of my social life. It would not be a place where I'd likely meet anyone to date. But I was welcomed in like family, grafted into this new city as though it could become my lasting home.

At St. Titus, I knew I was loved. It was a deeper, simpler, more stable kind of love than any I'd known from a church before. A love that was reinforced every time I walked to the altar rail, palms extended, and felt Mother Stephanie press the bread into my hand.

By fall break, I'd hit my stride. Each morning I brewed a pot of coffee, slathered toast in butter and jam, then sat at the table for two hours of writing—my book manuscript, which was due at the end of the semester, or freelance pieces to help pay the bills. Just before lunch, I walked the mile-and-a-half route to school, slowing my stride through the camellia blooms in Duke Gardens. My afternoons were split between class and homework in the library before an evening spent with friends.

I'd been invited to the mountains during the midsemester break for a gathering of people studying food and faith. At the campfire each night, we shared the ways we saw God at work: in gardens, around tables, in bread. As energized as I was by this growing community of leaders with interests similar to mine, I ended each day eager to return to Durham, to my friends.

Then, the Thursday after fall break, Claire pulled me aside after class. "So, um, Micah asked me out," she said.

The color drained from my face. "Oh, that's . . . that's great," I responded.

"Are you sure you're okay?" she asked.

"I'm happy for you," I replied, though it felt like the wind had been knocked out of me. While I'd been hesitant to hope for anything more than friendship for myself, it was refreshing to have fellow single friends for once. I wanted these budding relationships to remain the same.

The three of us sat together in the chapel each Monday evening for prayer, reciting the words of Mary's Magnificat week after week.

"You sure you're all right?" Claire asked as we left the chapel one night.

"Yep," I said quickly. But we both knew it wasn't true.

"Maybe you should get a dog," Gabrielle told me after I texted her with my laments. "I think it would help."

At Gabrielle's prompting, I began to research what it would look like to fit a pet into my life. I built a spreadsheet of the items I would need to buy—a collar, a kennel, bowls, food—and began researching breeds, deciding I could make it work in two months. I would finish the semester and wrap up the book I was writing. Then I'd look for a dog when I returned from Christmas back in Boston with my family.

"Maybe I should just go look now," I told my classmate Alice a few weeks before Thanksgiving break. "I could just see what's at the shelter to help me prepare."

"I'll come with you," she cheered.

That Friday afternoon, we drove to the Animal Protection Society of Durham.

"It's just to look," I reminded her as I took the exit onto East Club Boulevard. "I can't adopt quite yet."

The shelter was cold and sterile—at least, sterile in the sense that it was void of joy (though far from sterile if by *sterile* you mean clean). I plugged my nose against the acrid scent of urine that permeated the place and walked through the swinging doors to a warehouse lined with cages. Dog after dog yelped, scratching at the metal fencing, pleading for affection from Alice and me. It was a scene so gutting I nearly turned around and drove home. But then, across the room, our eyes met.

He sat silent in the crowd of yipping creatures, ears perked forward—each one as big as his face. Behind his big black pupils, I recognized a hollow longing, as though, like me, he couldn't bear more disappointment. The dogs around us faded away as I made my way toward him, my heart thumping, his tail wagging with excitement. He stuck his nose through the grates of the fence to sniff me and offer kisses, picking up his paws as if to dance.

"He's available for adoption tomorrow," the woman at the front desk said, breaking my reverie.

"There's just no way," I told Alice when it was time to go. "It's too much for me to handle right now."

***

"All . . . love is vast and inconvenient," Father Robert Farrar Capon says in his culinary treatise, *The Supper of the Lamb*. Love is the lifelong disquietude, as Capon describes it, of being made in the image of God.

"It is so much easier not to get involved—to thirst for nothing and no one," he writes. "But that, it seems to me, is neither human nor Divine. If we are to put up with all other bothers out of love, then no doubt we must put up with the bother of love itself and not just cut and run for cover when it comes."[3]

I went back to adopt the beagle the next day.

Though I was nervous about veering from the charted course, I decided to give love an inconvenient chance. A friend recommended I build a registry of my needs so I could be showered like the brides and expectant moms I'd showered over the years.

"You've made so many cakes," she said. "It's the least everyone can do."

It felt a bit self-indulgent. I had no qualms about pleading with God over my necessities, but when it came to expressing tangible needs to my friends, I worried I'd come across as begging for pity.

Even so, I swallowed my pride and filled out an online wish list with all the things I thought the dog could use. Then I sent it to a few friends.

Within hours, they'd purchased everything.

I named the pup Strudel as a nod to Father Capon, who describes the pastry as the triumph of elasticity. "It is in strudel dough that the glutinous properties of flour enter the new Jerusalem. . . . You will find it one of the great culinary absorptions of your life."[4]

The quiet, observational dog I'd met in the shelter soon turned out to be much more social and vocal than I expected. Strudel bayed out the window at any person who passed by, and he dug holes under the fence to escape the yard. He chewed up shoes and blankets, and he gnawed on wooden benches and shelves.

One evening when I took a break from reading to transfer a loaf of bread into the oven, I noticed the dough was missing.

Did I put it in the oven already? I thought.

I flicked on the oven light to check.

Empty.

That's when I noticed flour dusting the front of the cabinet and bits of dough stuck to the floor. I followed the trail of flour footprints all the way to my bed, where Strudel was splayed out, trying to get comfortable. He'd eaten it all—two pounds of dough.

For the next three hours his belly swelled, the stomach an ideal temperature for yeast. Frustrated as I was to be down a loaf, and a touch sympathetic to his pain, I couldn't help but chuckle at his pleading eyes.

I should have read Capon's treatise on strudel through to the end: "Admittedly, it's a lot of work," he writes. "Not to mention the wear and tear on the nerves."[5]

Despite his mischief, Strudel was an answer to prayer, a sign that God sees our needs and often meets them in unexpected ways.

"Struuuuuudel! Strudel!" I yelled down the street whenever I realized he'd escaped the backyard. He made the same rounds each time: across the street to greet the neighbor's longhaired pointer, then to the purple house with three pit bulls a few doors down. When the pit bulls shook the fence, he got scared away and trotted off to find any children playing on their front lawns. The neighbors knew my call.

"He's over here!" they'd yell in response, and we'd chat for a bit while the children played with Strudel's ears.

On days I didn't have class, when I spent my working hours at home writing, the conversations after Strudel's escape were my only human interaction.

On the nights I worked too late, Strudel covered my keyboard with his chin, reminding me to take a break. And on certain occasions, when I would cry over the ache of loneliness, Strudel curled up beside me and rested his head in my lap. He sighed and looked up at me with pleading eyes, then placed his paw over my hand.

In a way, I suppose Strudel's name is also a nod to God's offering of cake when I kept asking for bread. Strudel, the pastry, is a sort of cross between the two. Extravagant but with a satisfying chew.

⸻

"I want the cover to invoke the feeling of a dinner party," I told the publishing team. The book was about church meals, but I wanted to create a feeling more intimate than a fellowship hall. "I want the reader to feel like they're sitting at my table as soon as they see it."

"It's probably not going to feel like that unless you get a photo of your own table," the designer responded.

"Okay, that's fine," I said. "I will."

After I hung up, I asked a photographer friend if she would come to my house for a photo shoot.

"You want it to look full," she said. "Can you fit ten or so people around the table?"

I grinned, "Yep. Definitely."

"Awesome. Get a table runner and some candles. Make a big pot of soup, a few loaves of bread. A salad and a cheese board. We'll have about four hours of good light."

I invited my priest, her husband, and another couple from our church, along with Micah, Claire, Brett, and Haley. For four hours we posed at the table, eating cheese, sipping on soup, tearing loaves of bread, and clinking glasses. After dinner, we stood and circled the table, holding hands and praying the Lord's Prayer. In doing so, we marked the space as both holy and mundane.

Maybe this could be enough, I said to myself as the sun began to fall. *These people and this bread.*

I thought back to that moment at church just before I moved away from Boston.

If this is God's provision for the lonely, I thought, *then it will need to be enough for me.*

14

ON LONGING

In these holy mysteries . . . we are living members of the Body of your Son.

THE BOOK OF COMMON PRAYER,
"THE HOLY EUCHARIST"

DURHAM, NORTH CAROLINA

In Psalm 80, the psalmist laments, "You have fed them the bread of tears, made them drink tears in great measure."[1]

At first glance, I assume the psalmist is mourning because God has bestowed on the people a meal of tears instead of bread. I feel the emptiness of the psalmist's belly, the vacuous longing that seems it might crush a person from the inside, and I'm moved to tears as well. I know the pain of unmet longing.

But as I sit with the passage, I wonder if in fact the tears are not an alternative to bread but rather a presence as constant and nourishing as bread itself.

Tears alert us to our places of tenderness. They provide release when we have a need more visceral than words can convey. As a response to the ache in this world, tears are good. They allow us to be present to our physical and emotional well-being in a tangible way.

"Was it all in vain," writes poet Malcolm Guite in response to this psalm, "the way you tended us and nurtured us that we might bear good fruit in joy and peace?"[2]

The answer, I assume, is no: our tears and lamentations do not fall on deaf ears, despite the months or years it might seem that way. In the release that comes out of honest grief before the Lord, we are softened and shaped. The fruit of peace is washed in the salt of our tears.

———

Strudel nuzzled into my leg as I perused the list of therapists sent to me by the chaplain at divinity school. The list included options covered by the school's insurance plan and gave a small descriptor of each therapist.

One name caught my eye: Sister Chris, of the Immaculate Heart of Mary.

I wanted to see a therapist to talk through my experience of singleness, frustrated that none of my friends could relate. After years of disappointment, I'd shifted away from the assumption that I just hadn't met the right person yet. I was beginning to come to terms with the possibility that I could be single for life. If God didn't promise me a partner, but rather belonging through community, then I wanted to learn how to be okay—how to get rid of the pain of unmet longing.

What better support, I thought, than from someone who chose celibacy—someone who chose to refrain, of her own volition, from marriage to an earthly spouse in order to devote her life more fully to serving God.

"How do you do it?" I asked her in our first session. "How do you remain so content in your singleness?"

She paused for a moment, smiling and taking a deep breath.

"We all need intimacy," she said. "We need to be loved and known."

I nodded, pulling at the tissue in my hand.

"I've spoken to a lot of married couples who sit where you're sitting, and I can promise you I have more intimacy, I am more known by my fellow sisters, than some of the couples who come in here."

I complained that Protestant tradition doesn't offer any structure for that kind of intimacy. Maybe that was why happiness continued to elude me.

"I'm trying to build intergenerational relationships," I told her. "Hospitality—I think it's key. I really think it's the way God meets this need."

She nodded.

"But I'm still so lonely," I whispered, so my voice wouldn't crack.

She looked at me for a moment before answering. "Kendall, maybe you're not called to be single like me."

I sighed. This was not what I came to hear. I wanted someone to unlock the code to finding contentment in my unmarried state, someone who would help me shift from hollow longing to contented peace.

"Maybe your dissatisfaction suggests you're *supposed* to long for marriage and a family," she offered.

I wanted freedom from the burden of desire, and I wanted her to give me the tools to understand how to let go. Instead, she suggested I sit in my longing and ask what God was doing through it, right now.

"Do you want to be a mother?" my new friend Aminah, a doctoral student at Duke, asked from across the table. She'd been observing me as I played with her daughters while she prepared dinner. Aminah had a decade on me, and she understood how it felt to spend her twenties longing for a partner, facing ongoing disappointment in the dating realm. Then, in the span of a year, her life flipped around: she met her husband, and they married, got pregnant, moved to another state, and bought a house.

My eyes began to well with tears at her question. I tried not to allow myself to think about my longing for a family. Several of my friends had received PCOS diagnoses recently after struggling for years to conceive. As the belief that God would never answer my prayer for a partner took root, along with the growing awareness that my body might not be able to hold on to a pregnancy if given the chance, I learned to dam up hope of marriage and motherhood. By holding back hope, I thought I'd be able to hold back the intensity of my longing. Somehow the hollowness seemed more manageable than drowning in disappointment.

In some of my lonelier moments—late nights in my apartment, alone with Strudel—I scrolled through social media and tried to calculate at what age various friends had met their partners. I'd think back on the single women I looked up to in my teenage and college years—youth leaders, church members, fellow volunteers on the ship.

Sometimes it brought comfort to find that they'd met their significant other when they were close to my age, as though I'd discovered evidence that my own partner must be just around the corner. Sometimes it brought a twisted pride to know they were younger, as though it justified the intensity of my heartache and proved I'd earned the right to feel betrayed by God.

God has said no to the family I want, I told myself. Rather than exert any more energy pleading for a partner, I begged God to give me peace.

Aminah shifted the subject, which I was grateful for, as I didn't want to sob in the middle of their family dinner. As the meal went on, we talked about teaching and writing and, naturally, bread. We cleared the table and discussed my indecision over whether to pursue doctoral work; she heard my anxieties over the future—the same ones I'd been mulling over for the past few years. I held many dreams but struggled to understand how they might all piece together.

Her hands were deep in suds, washing dishes, when I said, "I just want to write and bake and teach!"

She reached over, taking my hands in her own, and replied, "And to be a mother. You are allowed to say it."

Something inside me broke open. That dam I'd so carefully constructed broke, and I could no longer ignore the intensity of my desire. I held in my tears until I reached the car, when I turned on the music she'd given me: an album of Advent music focused on themes of extended waiting.

The next day I embarked on a thirteen-hour road trip to visit my family for Christmas, and I wept on and off the entire way. The prayers and tears were more raw than those I'd shed during the spring of weddings. They flowed not just out of loneliness or disappointment but out of my anger at God and my anger at my lack of control over my dating life.

"Wait for the Lord, whose day is near," I sang with the Taizé chants on my playlist. "I waited for the Lord / God heard my cry."

"I've waited," I yelled, banging on my steering wheel as I wound up I-95 through Virginia. "But you're not listening!" I screamed.

The song turned: "My soul magnifies the Lord, my spirit rejoices in God / For He who is mighty has done great things."

I'd repeated these words while sitting next to Micah and Claire during evening prayer week after week, but they twisted within me in a new way on this trip—so aware that Mary was praising God for the child in her womb.

"You can do anything," I sobbed. "Why won't you step in here?"

I balled my fists, searching for release of some sort but out of words to convey the depth of my heartache. I'd leaned into the community God had put before me. I'd tried to make peace with the idea that I might never bear children or find a spouse. But as sweet as my friendships and church relationships were, the hollowness remained.

Over the course of that tearful Christmas drive, Sister Chris's words took on new meaning. As I allowed my tears and my anger to flow, I sensed that God might not be asking me to let go of my desire, challenging me to be content living without the family I wanted. My singleness was not a mathematical equation I could solve by calculating God's answers to other women's prayers. It was not a game I could win with the right amount of contentment. It was not a burden I needed to release so I could see the joy.

Rather, God was inviting me to feel the full intensity of my longing, to allow those longings to shape and soften me, as water softens the fibrous compounds in wheat. God was inviting me to weep and mourn the pain of unfulfilled desire without attempting to make sense of it all.

There was no assurance that doing so would be the key to unlocking my desire—in fact, it held the potential for deeper pain if my prayers remained unanswered. But learning to long also brought with it the freedom to hope, so I decided to give them both a try. The dams I'd built to block my sadness gave in the rest of the way. My emotions came over me in heavy waves. But I found a new tenderness there too.

In Christian tradition, one of the primary means of knowing God is by breaking. In the sacrament of the Eucharist, the breaking of the loaf marks the moment of mysterious transformation from ordinary bread into Jesus' Body. It was the breaking of bread that alerted the disciples of Christ's presence on the path to Emmaus. In the Gospel account, the disciples walked and talked with a stranger for hours about the perplexing accounts of Jesus' resurrection. Only when the stranger broke bread and extended it to them did they realize he was Jesus, the one who had been walking with them all along.

Breaking is a necessary aspect of remaking. It is the breaking that allows us to eat and, in our eating, to be transformed. It is the sharing of a broken loaf that binds us together in community.

In the collapse of my emotional dams, I felt hope and longing wash over me, transforming me. This breaking alerted me to the nearness of God in my weeping. It allowed me to see God not as a divine puppeteer holding me back from the good things I desired but as a tender mother holding me in her arms, her tears mingling with my own.

I began praying the words of Psalm 126:5, allowing the tears to flow: "Those who sow in tears will reap with cries of joy."

By the time I returned to Durham after Christmas, I decided it was time to begin baking at volume again. My hands longed for the feel of dough, for the opportunity to bring others joy through feeding. Though I still didn't know what my life would look like after graduation that spring, I knew the grounding I would find as I dug my hands through wheat. I sent emails to teachers, classmates, and friends, asking if they'd be interested in a bread share—a loaf a week for ten weeks, delivered straight to school. I could make fifteen loaves a day in my home kitchen, and I had the capacity to bake two times a week. By the time classes began in January, all thirty spots were full.

I mixed the flour and water by hand before bed, then awoke before the sun to begin shaping. Alone in my kitchen, I stretched and folded dough. Light began to crack through the window over my sink while I sang and swayed in time with the movements of my hands, my soundtrack an album of songs focused on the holiness of work:

> Your labor is not in vain
>
> Though the ground underneath you is cursed and stained[3]

The loaves rose while I read and showered, integrating my rhythms of work, study, and daily life, and they baked and cooled just in time for me to head to school. As in the days before I left for the ship, the routine brought solace to my racing mind.

I prayed for guidance for the months ahead, after graduation. In addition to grounding me as I sought direction, the loaves themselves provided a path forward. I could grow the bread share, allowing me to balance both baking and writing—the baking enabling my writing, and my writing bringing meaning to the loaves.

The business took form in my mind, simpler than the bakery I'd envisioned in my ship days. I would partner with churches as pickup locations, making their Communion bread as thanks for participating. In these simple rhythms, this share would connect the bread broken on Sunday morning to the bread consumed all through the week.

The owner of a local popsicle shop and café, a middle-aged single woman who'd paid me to develop recipes for her shop, offered access to her kitchen whenever I was ready as well as support in developing my business plan. Each week, as I shaped and danced and sang, barefoot in my kitchen, the vision for this bakery clicked into place a bit more. I played the same album again and again, allowing the words to permeate my body, to drive the choreography of my shaping, and in so doing, to reframe my vision of what it meant to live out my vocation.

> *He is moving in our hands and feet to bless*
> *In the fields of the Lord our work is rest* [4]

I was tired of the restlessness, tired of the loneliness, tired of the years of unmet longing. But in this bread, my work could be rest.

The etymology of the word *companion* means a person who breaks bread with another. At one time it referenced social hierarchy: the person you broke bread with was the person who shared your social class. The word itself also holds the potential to subvert its intended meaning, connoting relationships that cross such divides and pointing to the power of bread to build relationships in unexpected ways.

I thought back to the Companion Bakery in Saint Louis that donated leftovers to my church when I was in high school. I was reminded of the children running around, munching on bagels, while adults chatted. That community was the first place I'd witnessed the desire to see God's intergenerational, cross-cultural, multilingual Kingdom brought to bear. The bread formed the community in both sacrament and lived experience. With that community in mind, I chose the name for my new venture: Companion Bread Share.

"I don't really know how to pray anymore," I told Emily and Gabrielle one night at the end of February. "For a partner, I mean." Rain pattered against the windshield as I drove east down H Street in Washington, DC.

We'd met up for a weekend reunion, reminiscing over our Chez Heureuse days and celebrating the strides we'd made in our careers since then: Emily had just finished graduate school and accepted a job at a top Boston architecture firm. Gabrielle was rounding out a project at the Folger Shakespeare Library in DC. I was making plans to grow Companion, moving into the popsicle shop kitchen after graduation. As our final day together drew to a close, I burst into tears. "I'm tired. I think maybe God does want to answer my prayers, but . . . I just don't know what to say anymore."

"Is it weird if we pray over you?" Emily asked. "I think it would be good for you to hear the prayers of someone else."

I pulled over in front of Whole Foods, where Gabrielle ran inside to grab a few pints of ice cream. Emily and I sat in silence while we waited, listening to the rain. We returned to our room, ice cream in hand, and sat down on one of the beds, our heads resting on one another's shoulders as Gabrielle and Emily alternated between praying and eating spoonfuls of black raspberry chip.

"God, you know Kendall has cried and prayed for years," Emily said. "We want to see her receive the love and care she desires."

"Someone who values hospitality, who is thoughtful and kind," Gabrielle added. "Someone who reads deeply and enjoys theology talk, though, let's be real—it's probably better if he's not an academic. Or even a pastor. That's a bit much."

"A really great beard is important too," Emily said, stifling a laugh. "Kendall. You know it's true."

I sighed. She wasn't wrong.

I listened to these friends cling to God on my behalf, trusting that God would provide in the most specific of ways. They knew me in the intimate manner Sister Chris described. They'd observed me and heard me, and they expressed my desires to God with more particularity than I knew how to describe on my own. As they prayed and I cried and we all spooned our pints of ice cream, a small image floated into my mind, like a quiet promise from God. In it, I was cradling a child. I clung to that picture in the days ahead, an image that held my hope together with my as yet unmet longing. The next morning I drove home, down I-95 through Virginia, this time buoyed by the hope of my friends.

The following weekend I made a birthday cake for a friend, decorated like a narwhal, at her request. I arrived late to the party, sneaking in through the back door to slip the cake onto the dessert table.

"Wow, did you make that?" someone asked from behind me. I turned around to see a tall man with a black beard smiling at the cake.

"I did!" I said nervously, racking my brain for ways to flirt—a skill I had still not mastered.

"I'm William," he said, extending a hand to shake. "I'm taking some theology courses as a break during med school."

"So . . . what do you know about William?" I texted Claire as I left the party. "Because, um, very cute."

I texted Gabrielle and Emily next: "Y'all won't believe this guy I just met."

Over the coming weeks I began to see William in the hallways between classes. I went to campus early and stayed late at the library, hoping for extra chances to run into him. In the one class we shared, I noticed he sat increasingly closer to me.

"Hey, how's your week going?" he asked one morning as class ended. He took the longer route out of the room, which conveniently allowed him to walk right past me. I spilled my coffee and stumbled over my words as I tried to respond.

Mutual friends began inviting us both to dinners and then left us to chat while they cleared the dishes. I learned that in college he'd attended the church that first planted my high school congregation, New City. He told me about the ways the church had shaped him and formed his love for theology. I commented on his band T-shirts—all of which happened to be the few bands I knew.

I was smitten. And I was certain that this was, at last, God's answer to my prayer. After a month, at the encouragement of Emily and Gabrielle, I asked him out.

"Would you be up for drinks one day next week?" I texted after we left another dinner with friends.

"I'd love that!" he responded.

We made plans to meet at my favorite brewery. I borrowed a dress from a friend and fiddled with my makeup all afternoon. For three hours, we laughed and drank and talked, and then we hugged goodbye.

"I don't talk to anyone for three hours unless I'm interested," a male friend told me in response to the date.

"Same, for sure," another responded.

"That seems really good!" said a third.

Pushing aside the memory of previous heartbreaks, I allowed myself to hope that things would be different this time. Then, for several days, silence.

"I'm so sorry," William told me after a week went by. "I'm just not interested in anything more."

I yelled at God from the kitchen, frightening Strudel, who only wanted to comfort me. I wept on the phone with friends who had no words to say.

"It feels like God has crushed me," I said. "Like God taught me to hope and then punched me all the way back down."

William was tender with his words, which made me admire him all the more and kept me from being angry at him the way I wanted to be. His kindness, even in his rejection, drew me to him, making it all the harder to know my affection wasn't returned.

Instead, I focused my disappointment on God.

"Is there anyone among you who, if your child asks for bread, will give a stone?" Jesus asks in Matthew 7:9 (NRSV).

"You would," I cried after reading the verse. "You just did."

A few weeks later, I received an email from my apartment property manager: "We'll be raising your rent by $125 a month for the coming year."

My mouth dropped open when I read the number—four times the rent increase of the year before. This was the maximum amount they could legally raise the rent of a current tenant. Committed to launching Companion Bread Share and aware of the financial risk involved, I begged the manager to reconsider.

"I'm self-employed; I run a business in this neighborhood. I can't afford this kind of increase. Is there anything you can do?"

They responded with a firm no, listing the apartment for an even higher price the next day.

"I think I'm going to have to find roommates," I complained to Emily and Gabrielle. "It's so expensive to live life on your own."

Before moving, I decorated one last cake in the kitchen: a four-tiered wedding cake for Micah and Claire.

"I'm tired of making decisions by myself," I complained to Alice at the wedding. I was overcome by the sense of unmooring that accompanied the spring of weddings two years before.

"Oh, you're still so young—don't worry," she responded.

"I'm not worried," I snapped. "Just alone."

Over the following months, the image I clung to as a sign of hope shifted in my mind. Perhaps it wasn't a child I cradled but a loaf, like the Panera woman whose image I'd studied all those years before. Bread made to break, to share with others—companions joined together to carry the weight of bellies empty in the face of great desire. Together we could eat and pray that God would be present with us in our pain.

I couldn't know whether I'd sustain a child with my own body, but with the gift of baking, I could certainly feed others.

15

ON CONTENTMENT

Let us go forth into the world, rejoicing in the power of the Spirit.

THE BOOK OF COMMON PRAYER,
"THE HOLY EUCHARIST"

DURHAM, NORTH CAROLINA

Prior to Vatican II, a major moment of reform in the Roman Catholic Church, the sacrament of baptism included the practice of placing salt on a baby's tongue. With its ability to purify and preserve food, salt symbolized protection for the baptized against the corruption of sin. The practice was rooted in the actions of the prophet Elisha, who poured salt into a spring to purify it. "I have healed this water," he says, speaking for the Lord. "Never again will it cause death or make the land unproductive."[1]

In addition to preserving food, salt opens taste receptors to subtle nuances of sweet and savory notes in food while also muting bitterness. The human body needs sodium chloride to survive, so there's a biological reason that our brains get excited over the taste of salt too.

To balance the flavors of a dish, a cook uses salt, along with acid and fat. The proper alignment of these elements is similar to striking a chord in music. Once aligned, none of the elements can be tasted on their own; rather, they work together to amplify the other flavors present in the dish. Salt plays a vital role in this dynamic, preparing the tongue to perceive the natural sweetness and nuances. In bread, salt serves a chemical function in addition to improving taste. It slows down yeast, forcing it to work through the dough at a more reasonable pace.

Jesus tells us that we are the salt of the earth. It's a role that sounds mundane, but in fact, it's a role of great worth: to stand against corruption and to mute bitterness. To bring slowness, balance, and rest. And to elevate the goodness of one's surrounding community.

I backed my Subaru up to the loading area at Fullsteam Brewery, unloading two bins of loaves I'd made using the grains left over from their Paycheck Pilsner.

"Your table's over here!" the events manager directed, pointing to a spot between a kombucha brewer and a screen printer. I spread out a white tablecloth and then balanced wooden crates filled with cookies and bread, writing my prices on a small chalkboard. At the corner of the table, I placed an antique loaf tin lined with parchment and filled with sample bites of bread.

The International Women's Day market was Companion's first appearance at a market. The brewery invited a dozen women-owned businesses to the event, where they expected a crowd of five hundred customers. Most of the vendors knew one another, having met at other markets across town. But they were excited to welcome a newcomer to the scene, coming over to inspect my table and suggest some kind of trade.

"Would you like a bag of homemade dog treats in exchange for a loaf?" one vendor asked.

"I'd love some cookies. Can I offer you a bouquet of flowers?" suggested another.

The bread share was a year old at this point, if you count the months

I baked from my home kitchen and distributed loaves at school. The jump from a home-based operation during graduate school into a full-scale operation, functioning out of a professional kitchen, was more strenuous than I'd expected. At first the growth didn't come at the rate I'd hoped for, and the increasing expenses subsumed any revenue I made. Then the holidays brought an influx of orders I wasn't prepared to handle, and I worried I'd outgrow the popsicle shop. By February, though, our sales had dropped again.

"Diversify," my mentor urged. "You've got to offer more than bread."

Despite the stress of slow growth, I was having fun. As I branched out to breakfast pastries, cookies, and quick breads, I built networks with coffee shops that were interested in serving my wares. I booked tables at a series of spring markets, this Women's Day market the first among them, and started conversations with a handful of farmers who wanted to offer bread with their weekly produce subscription box. I didn't have a sign or an elaborate setup for my table yet, so the samples would have to sell themselves this first time around.

"What's spent barley bread?" customers asked as they walked by, providing me the opportunity to share how the loaves were made using the remnants from the beer in their hands. I'd picked up the barley from the brewmaster a few days earlier after he'd soaked up all its natural sugars to create the base for beer. I dehydrated the sugarless barley for two hours in the oven before grinding it down to a flour that I mixed into dough that fermented for eighteen hours in the fridge. The barley made for a great story, in addition to a tasty loaf.

Rumors of a virus had been circulating for the past few weeks. I read about government-imposed lockdowns in other countries—first China, then Italy. Some folks worried the lockdowns would happen stateside, too, though I was so focused on Companion's growth that I didn't really register this news.

"I'm a bit nervous about this virus," my mom had told me as she left for the airport in late January, heading to Texas to say goodbye to Gramma Ruth, who was in a coma after a stroke.

"Oh, don't worry," I consoled her, worried she was subjecting herself to sensationalized stories.

A week later, after I returned home from Texas for the funeral, I bought a bag of beans and a jar of peanut butter. *Just in case,* I thought. *It will be good to have a few things on hand.* I bought some spaghetti noodles a few days after that.

By the time of the Women's Day market, the rumors had morphed into warnings, like the eerie stillness just before a tsunami breaks over land. As customers dropped bits of bread into their palms using a pair of plastic tongs, I wondered if the samples were a bad idea. Potential for viral spread aside, though, they worked. Almost everyone who tried some came back for more, remarking on the depth of flavor and the chewy crumb.

The customer interactions energized me. I loved seeing the looks on peoples' faces, surprised a loaf could hold so much depth. I enjoyed telling the story about how Companion began, about the vision for community shaped around simple bread. The bustling market brought as much joy as the hours alone in the kitchen. I looked forward to the rest of the markets throughout the spring.

Then, the next day, a local priest called me to cancel a large order. The church meal he'd planned to use it for was no longer taking place.

"We're closing our doors for at least two weeks," he told me over the phone after offering to pay me for the order despite the cancelation.

The day after that, the governor announced a state of emergency in North Carolina. I was sitting at my hundred-year-old table, tracking Companion's slow growth, when I received the alert by phone.

I typed a quick email for my customers: "Stock up on bread and cookies!" I wrote, worried that rumors of a total lockdown might come true.

After leaving my beloved duplex the previous fall, I'd found a house large enough to share with two other people, plus a couch and my table.

"Kendall, this home is insane," Brett said as we carried the couch up the stairs. "Look at that wall of windows!"

"Did you see the magnolia out back?" Haley asked. "I'd drink my coffee on that porch every day."

Though the house was beautiful, I struggled to appreciate it. I was sad to have left my old neighbors behind, sad to give up living alone.

"Yeah, I know." I sighed. "I just hope I can find decent roommates."

I'd listed the house on various message boards, hoping to connect with the right folks, but so far the options had been slim. Everyone I'd met was fresh out of college, an age gap that felt too far to bridge.

"I'm just not sure there are any other single women in this city my age," I said, rolling my eyes. "I know it sounds crazy, but we are in the South, after all. If they do exist, they probably want to live alone, like me."

After a week, I received a message that sounded oddly familiar:

"Hi, I'm Emily. I'm an architect moving from Charlottesville, Virginia."

It was almost exactly the same email I'd received years before, when I moved into Chez Heureuse. I called Emily to ask why she was playing this joke on me when she knew how stressed I was about my housing. I hadn't lived with a roommate since her wedding, which left my bar for roommates quite high.

"It's not me!" the original Emily promised with a laugh. "But she sounds great."

When the governor announced a state of emergency, Emily—the second one—and I began developing a plan. We'd lived together for six months by then, our friendship forming slowly on the few evenings we were both home at the same time.

"Should we just share food?" she asked.

It would only be the two of us at the house—our third roommate moved back to her parents' house when rumors of a lockdown spread— so we decided we might as well split cooking duties.

"Should we buy some games?" I asked.

"I've been wanting to learn to count cards," Emily responded. "You know, like for blackjack." She didn't gamble—she just liked the idea of acquiring the skill, and the looming lockdown seemed like a decent time to learn.

"I'm going to try my hand at sewing," I added.

We drove to Target, Trader Joe's, and the craft store, loading the car with anything we might need to make it through the coming weeks. I chuckled at the bare shelves where flour used to be.

"Is everyone going to learn how to bake now?" I asked.

Once we'd built up our own supply of wares, we made a final stop: the restaurant supply store, where I could load up on fifty-pound bags of flour in the hope that Companion might grow despite the looming unknowns.

Up to that point, our shopping had had an air of giddiness, like the excitement of kids the night before a snow day—except that it would last for weeks and we wouldn't have to shovel in the cold. At Restaurant Depot, though, the tone changed, like a hospital waiting room pulsing with the knowledge that some of us would emerge grieving the loss of a loved one (or perhaps a business), and some of us would emerge battered but okay.

I piled bags of flour onto my cart, calculating how long they would last. I figured I could make sixty-five loaves per bag. Six bags would have to do.

We loaded three hundred pounds of flour into my trunk and drove home.

"Most of those folks won't have a business by the time this is through," I said.

Emily looked over with half a smile.

"*I* might not have a business," I added.

⸻

Everyone did, in fact, learn how to bake in the weeks ahead. Men and women across the country sought solace by putting their hands in dough. It became a sort of joke—all the people who leaned into sourdough, striving for grounding, hoping to work through the stress of these pandemic days. Flour distributors were unable to keep up with the new demand amid their own shutdowns.

I shouldn't have been surprised, though—this drive was primal, a need to connect with generations who'd gone before us and survived. Bread was doing precisely what it had long been used to do.

Novice bakers reached out to ask me for tips for their sourdough starters. In addition to typing up documents about feeding cycles and various kinds of grains, I encouraged them to use the rhythm as a form of prayer. I resonated with the guttural urge that compelled them to bake; I wanted them to understand it might be cliché, but it's good.

I, too, needed a place to channel my anxious energy. I was struggling against the drive to press full speed ahead when the future felt amorphous. I was spurred by the creative challenge of adapting my business but frustrated that I couldn't plan more than a week ahead, if that.

Since Companion opened, I'd been searching for a way to offer loaves to community members who couldn't afford them, as well as a way for customers to subsidize those loaves. This donation-loaf idea embodied what I envisioned Companion to be: relationships formed through the sharing of bread, providing for one another's needs.

After connecting with local churches and food distribution programs, I added a donation-loaf product to our order form. Loved ones from across the country who wanted to support Companion seized the opportunity to participate in this way. Soon I was baking 120 loaves each baking cycle, delivering loaves to doorsteps all around the city every Thursday and then dropping off bags of bread at food banks on Fridays.

I drew maps of the city, plotting out delivery points and growing intimately acquainted with all the streets of my town. The drive was eerie, with those once-bustling streets now void of people. But it was worshipful, too.

"Grant protection to the nurses and doctors," I whispered as I pulled away from my commercial kitchen and drove past Duke hospital. "And an abundance of energy, too."

"God, please help them stay afloat!" I said as I drove past a café whose owners I knew.

I crossed myself as ambulances passed by and handed extra loaves to men and women begging for food on the side of the road.

Then I headed home, where more customers would stop by to pick up their loaves. They pulled into the gravel drive all afternoon to retrieve their orders from a plastic bin, waving to me through the living room window while Strudel howled hello. When the last loaf was gone and Emily's workday was finished, we headed to the back porch under the shade of the magnolia tree while Strudel watched the squirrels skitter across the yard. We talked about our families, our faith, our dreams.

It was fun. Almost. This rhythm of baking and praying; of Emily, Strudel, and me building our quarantine home. It was the type of companionship I'd been longing for—found not through a romantic partner, but through the simple and intimate rhythms of friendship formed at the table, in the face of grief.

Despite the tragedies unfurling around the world, I was, for the moment, happy. It wasn't a happiness I expected to last in any profound way, but it was a taste, and that taste was good.

Over time I found a market among those who had acquired a taste for fresh bread in the early sourdough craze but found the process too much to keep up on their own. I also found a market among those who wanted some kind of rhythm to ground them week after week, some touchpoint to mark the passing of the days. And I found a market among folks who missed their Sunday-morning community—those who craved bread at a level deeper than they could comprehend. More than bread, they craved Christ's Body.

Though every church handled the dispersion of the elements differently, my own held to the belief that the Eucharist is reserved for times we're together in body, knit together through our physical proximity, sharing the bread blessed and broken by the words and hands of the priest.

Churches of all denominations and traditions found their convictions challenged and shaped by this modern pandemic in which congregations were physically separate yet virtually connected. Some emphasized the need, all the more, for their communities to be bonded across time and space—offering blessings over church members' home-baked bread via computer screen. Others offered a drive-through version of the sacrament, preserving the priestly role while meeting the hunger for bread, even when the hunger for Communion itself couldn't be filled.

The more I baked and the more I saw others baking too, the more I hungered for the small wafer I missed each Sunday morning. Despite the grounding I found in baking and feeding, I ached for the touch of my congregation as we held hands to sing the Lord's Prayer. I ached for the bread I was missing, the bites shared on Sunday morning.

I felt in my hands and my empty belly that those bites had never been just about the bread. They were about the global, historical community they united me to, and they were about the people standing beside me too.

"There's a priest wandering around outside my shop," my mentor yelled into the kitchen of the popsicle shop, where I was packaging loaves. "I assume she's looking for you."

I hadn't seen Reverend Stephanie in four months, since the Sunday I slipped out of the service, my dress dusted in flour, to set up my table at the Women's Day market, unaware that it would be my final Sunday for a while.

I rolled a rickety cart piled with bread from the kitchen to the parking lot.

"It's so good to see you!" I exclaimed, holding back tears as soon as I saw her standing six feet away.

In the months after churches closed down, I kept in touch with the pastors I'd met while researching church meals, curious how they would translate their dinner services into a virtual setting. At their prompting, I developed resources for communities of all sizes to host virtual worship services as meals—each person sitting at their own dining table, connected through a screen and a shared soup recipe.

The agape meal, or "love feast," is a tradition passed down from the Moravian church. The meal is intended to bind a community together when the absence of a pastor or priest prevents them from celebrating Communion. In the separation wrought by the pandemic, communities wanted not for a pastor or a priest but for the ability to gather in person. The virtual agape meal I designed functioned in a similar manner to the traditional one, addressing the need for deep community and fellowship with one another, even if done in a less-than-satisfying way.

As these resources began circulating through churches from various denominations, local congregations asked if they could buy bread for their virtual services. A pastor would pick up a batch of Companion loaves and then drive around town to distribute them to each of their members before they gathered online to break bread across a screen. While I still ached for the Sunday table, baking for these meals got me one step closer.

On the day Reverend Stephanie came to pick up loaves, I had the opportunity to bake for my own church community—the people I hadn't seen in four months, except for a handful of faces that appeared on the recorded service each Sunday morning.

St. Titus had ordered twenty-five loaves to break over a virtual meal that evening. I prayed for each family by name as I shaped the bread: against illness and loneliness, for a satisfying moment of communion in the midst of our hunger for Holy Communion as we met online to share loaves formed from a single batch of dough.

I left the cart in the middle of the parking lot and then stepped six feet away, leaving enough distance for Reverend Stephanie to pick up the loaves herself. This dance had become strangely familiar by that point. We said goodbye, our smiles registered only through our eyes, as masks covered the rest of our faces.

"See you tonight," she said, "I hope you are well."

A few hours later, we exchanged smiles again, this time with faces exposed from the safety of our computer screens. One by one, more households joined the call. It was an odd but intimate experience, being welcomed into everyone's kitchens, breaking bread in one another's homes as the early church had. Kind of. We took turns reading Scripture, praying aloud the liturgy for evening prayer from *The Book of Common Prayer*, along with text from the *Didache*. "As this grain was scattered upon the fields and, being gathered together, became one, so may your church be gathered together from the ends of the earth into your kingdom," we said, in a stilted attempt at unison, our microphones picking up one voice at a time.[2]

I watched as each household tore open their loaves, eyes lighting up as the scent filled the room. The Woodards topped slices with Camembert. The Furges family smeared theirs with butter.

"I'm sorry—I couldn't wait until the service. I already ate half of mine plain," Ms. Gloria said, chuckling.

When the laughter subsided, I encouraged the gathered congregation to continue enjoying their meal while I preached. "We gather tonight feeling the collective weight of isolation," I began. "Our separation deepens our longing for Communion. This strange method of gathering might not appease our desire to be together in body, but it offers us something to cling to while we wait."

Each time I distributed loaves for a virtual agape meal, I sensed that, in a way, this unsatisfying answer is what Communion itself always offers. This bread and this wine are a gift from God—a promise of God's commitment to healing, a promise to restore all things and bring us to the day when there will be no more death and no more mourning. Through this meal, God also shapes us into a community that reflects the work God is doing in the world. It shapes us as individuals; it teaches us to care for one another and meet one another's needs. But as it shapes us and fills us, it also trains us to hunger for God's healing all the more. It offers us something to hold on to until the day Christ comes again. It is enough but, by its very nature, leaves us wanting.

This tension echoed my longing for marriage combined with my joy in companionship with friends: I was filled, and at the same time, I was not. Meanwhile, the hunger itself—and the unmet longing—shaped me too. Even when my hands were submerged in dough for hours on end, I was learning to hope for the day of Christ's return while remaining grounded in the present moment.

It was another three months before my church offered the sacrament instead of this virtual approximation. The crowd was small, with many of our congregants considered too high risk to attend. We gathered outside, in the parking lot, wearing masks and carrying our own chairs from home to avoid spreading germs.

One by one, we received the bread, dropped into our palms with silver tongs—no wine, as dipping the wafers could contribute to more spread. Each of us slipped the cracker under our masks and chewed.

After the service, we exchanged greetings from six feet away, but the conviviality that typically accompanied our post-service conversation was missing. We couldn't hug or shake hands or even stand close enough to hold a naturally flowing conversation.

I climbed into my car and headed home, tears of relief and sadness welling in my eyes. I'd hungered for this bite—and for the community that went with it. It was what I needed, but not enough at all.

⸺

In the span of a few months, Companion received the funds to donate one thousand loaves of bread. I distributed hundreds more through churches around town that wanted to meet the spiritual and communal needs of their congregation in some tangible way.

Each week, I baked alone in the popsicle shop kitchen, shaping and singing and praying. Though I was grateful to witness the communal momentum around this bread, I was uncomfortable with the praise from those who felt like Companion was doing such good work. While I was excited to feed my community, I was also desperate to save my business. And I needed to bake to feel sane.

I'd drafted a solution that met my needs by meeting the needs of others, but I hardly felt like a saint. I felt almost selfish, really—this plan too simple to be worth any measure of praise.

But maybe this is how God intends for us to flourish and thrive: by noticing the small, simple ways our own needs and offerings fit together. When community is formed, relationships are built where it's safe to express our points of hunger, loneliness, and longing. Then our eyes are opened to the ways our own deep pain and our search for healing can reveal the path toward healing for one another as well.

I think back on my younger self, so concerned about discerning what God wanted me to do. I longed to make a difference in the world in some magnificent way. But the Kingdom of God is like yeast, which a woman mixed into three measures of flour. The work was hard, and her strength was impressive, but the process was simple, too. She mixed, and the yeast slowly worked its way through the dough, transforming it as it feasted and filled its own insatiable need.

In those days when we were physically separated from one another, God asked me to do small, simple tasks again and again, saving my business and meeting my own desire to bake. In the meantime, God used this bread to meet the needs of others as well.

The Kingdom of God is like yeast, slowly transforming the wheat. But we are the salt, developing strength and flavor to draw out the nuances already present in the dough.

Salt is so simple, so mundane. As is bread. But it's in these small, ordinary elements that God meets us, transforms us, and sends us out to transform the communities we're in.

To be the salt of the earth is small. It's simple, mundane.

But maybe a mundane, salt-of-the-earth kind of life is all we really need.

16

ON HOPE

DURHAM, NORTH CAROLINA

"If all laboured for their bread and no more, then there would be enough food and enough leisure for all," Mahatma Gandhi wrote in protest against British control.[1] In 1930 Gandhi marched thousands of Indians more than two hundred miles to the shores of the Arabian Sea to acquire salt in protest of Britain's regulation of salt production and heavy salt tax. This nonviolent act of resistance led to more protests and tens of thousands of arrests, but it paved the way for freedom from imperialist rule.[2]

Gandhi wasn't the first person to use salt as means of protecting the vulnerable against greedy rulers. Throughout history, wars have been fought against countries that attempt to limit the public's access to salt—like the Italian Salt War in the 1480s or the El Paso Salt War of 1877.

In the ancient world, Roman soldiers were paid, in part, with salt. The allowance, called a *salarium*, was the root of the contemporary term *salary*.[3]

Salt is as precious as daily bread. It's worth risking arrest, even death, to protect against dictators who would try to take it away. The freedom to collect salt from the ocean, from salt flats, or from mines is a freedom for which many have paid with their lives.

A simple salt-of-the-earth kind of life is shaped by the prayer for daily bread—in trust that God will continue to provide just what we need to do the work we're called to do.

"I can't live like this anymore," I wrote on a piece of scrap paper while on a plane back to Durham. I'd been visiting my older sister, Alyssa, in Denver—one of the first times I'd gone out of town since the pandemic had hit. For months, time had been a blur, measured by the intervals between bake days, by car rides around town as I dropped off bread on the porches of faithful customers.

The change of scenery and the break in routine snapped me into an awareness of the toll the year had taken on my body. *God, something has to change.*

My arms and back ached from the bake a few days before. I'd slept eleven hours each night of my stay in Colorado, through the screams of my infant nephew in the next room. I could hardly finish a conversation without thinking about Companion. There was the pie event scheduled for the next weekend, intended to drum up interest in Thanksgiving orders. The Christmas offerings I would ship around the country. The holiday markets I could attend, if I wasn't too late to apply—an attempt to make up for all the events that had been canceled the previous spring. My brain churned night and day. As much as I wanted to, I couldn't turn it off.

I'd mapped out what I could manage to bake over the holidays, along with the revenue I would need in order to pay my bills and my taxes. Before the weekend escape to Colorado, I'd survived by pushing myself one week at a time. I just needed to make it through the end of the year, and then I could rest, I told myself. I held the stress in my shoulders and my upper back, but it was now starting to creep down my spine and into my hips, too.

After the first big wave of the pandemic subsided over the summer, the economic stress kicked in. Customers began to tighten their finances, and sales fluctuated week by week. Though I was baking as much as my body could handle, the weekly revenue didn't reflect all the labor. I tried to trust God with the details of the business, to take joy in each small sign of growth. *If I can push through the holiday season,* I thought, *I'll be okay.*

I knew this work was what God had prepared me to do, and though I was exhausted, I was giddy with anticipation about the year to come. I'd be able to bake and write and support others through my baking— connecting head, heart, hands, and home, while (hopefully) slowing the pace of my life.

After scribbling more pleas to God, listing the specific details that needed to come together, I wrote a recipe for bread in the form of a prayer (which can be found in the appendix). Drawing from the evening prayer liturgy in *The Book of Common Prayer*, I created a liturgy that doubled as instructions for baking—a prayer to be expressed through the Body and through words when my own words weren't enough.

Even from my seat on a plane somewhere over Missouri, I could feel the bread prayer at work, permeating my body.

Our strengths and weaknesses are often two sides of the same coin. Learning to lean into our strength requires that we recognize how it functions as a weakness, too. For me, that strength looks like being grounded and providing a solid footing for others. But under stress, it can look more like a quest for control.

The dance between trusting God and leaning into my ability to get things done feels like getting to know the character of bread. Sometimes

God asks me to do something illogical, and sometimes I ask illogical things of God—and sometimes I can't tell which way the crazy goes. As with baking, I learn to attune myself to the environment around me, feeling for the places of resistance in the dough. Sometimes these places are signs of strength, and sometimes they're signs of exhaustion—often they're both at once. It takes practice and several rounds of failure to learn how to respond to the bread accordingly.

While a failed loaf is, of course, disappointing, it brings the baker one step closer to a better batch. I remind myself of this whenever I stumble over the steps in this waltz of trusting God—the God who made me ambitious and eager, and also finite and in need of rest.

I was trying to trust that, as long as I took the next step down the path God laid before me, God would provide for my emotional, financial, and physical needs. I had seen God do just that, time and time again, even when I let my stress overwhelm me.

Back home in Durham, I went to bed willing myself to trust God in this season.

The next day I woke to a text from my mentor, the owner of the kitchen space I used. "Can we talk tomorrow?" she asked.

Driving to work, I had a sense that the conversation wouldn't end well. I was worried I'd just about overstayed my welcome—I was outgrowing the space but couldn't yet afford a space of my own. Our agreement was fuzzy, each of us unsure how to clarify the bounds of the relationship, and as a result, both of us were perpetually afraid we'd be taken advantage of.

Just minutes into the interaction, I could see that Companion would not be able to stay.

"I'll have to close," I said, the gravity of the situation becoming apparent through my words before I'd fully grasped them in my mind.

We agreed to terms that allowed me to use the space through the holidays so I could save a little and figure out my next steps. I looked into other facilities whose kitchens were more conducive to the volume of bread I was making, but every day the work wore my body down more. By the time I got home, my back was too sore for daily tasks. On my days off, I was too exhausted to stay awake. Soon I began to experience shooting pain through my fingers, and I'd wake up each morning with numb hands. Midway through mixing, I'd lose the ability to grip a spoon. My stress and my tendency to overwork had hit a breaking point.

I could not go on.

Months before, I'd booked a weekend visit to Margarita, who was now living with her husband and two-year-old son in San Juan, Puerto Rico. With airline points set to expire by the end of the year, I was trying to visit loved ones as best I could with the current travel restrictions. When I booked the trip, I knew I needed the escape—even if the journey put me at high risk of getting sick—but at the time I couldn't have projected how much I'd need to be with a friend that weekend. Especially one who had been by my side throughout adulthood and could remind me of God's faithfulness over more than a decade.

We waded in the water as her son, Joaquin, dug through the sand, the salty water stinging our legs.

"There's just something so isolating about making decisions on my own," I said as my feet sunk in the silt. "I'm tired of it."

"I'm sure," Margarita responded. "I can't really imagine."

"Most of the time I'm confident about the projects I'm taking on— like it's exactly what I'm in this world to do." I sighed. "But I can't do them if my basic needs aren't met. And I just don't know if I can really trust God to step in."

She looked at me gently as I averted my eyes. "Well, I think we know that's not true," Margarita replied. "God wants to take care of you, Kendall. And if God gave you this work, he'll make a way."

"Yeah, I'm just sad, frankly." I sighed.

"And that's okay."

"How about you?" I asked, unsure how to broach her own grief— infertility after her first pregnancy, followed by a miscarriage just a few months before.

"Loss is hard," she replied. "And really lonely."

There's a sweetness to friendship that has journeyed together through seasons of celebration and grief. In some ways, our lives had unfolded along similar lines—dancing, writing, studying theology, knowing longing and grief, living in bodies that didn't function the way we wanted them to. And in other ways they'd diverged—marriage and motherhood for her, and singleness and business ownership for me. Both our similarities and differences enabled us to be present for each another in unique ways.

Later that night we picked up the conversation from the beach.

"I don't feel like I can just . . . find another job," I shared. "I've always spread myself too thin. I feel like there's writing I'm still supposed to do."

"You're doing what you've always wanted to do," she told me. "You've got writing, and you've got bread."

Though I wanted to keep forcing the next steps of the waltz, when it came down to it, I knew God's character well enough to trust that I could wait for guidance about what was to come. But I also knew the sadness that came with letting go. While God's plan might be tender, loving, and good, the disappointment on the way to get there is real.

"I know God's inviting me to slow down," I told her. "But I'm afraid God's going to ask me to let it all go. My writing. My teaching. Everything. I've given up too much already."

"If he does, you'll be ready," she replied. "Just like you're sad to let go of Companion, but also ready."

I waited a few more weeks before announcing Companion's closure to my customers, holding on just a little longer. Some of my regulars had begun to advertise on my behalf in their neighborhoods, drumming up dozens of pie and dinner roll sales for Thanksgiving.

"I'm so excited about your business!" a few of them said when they came to pick up their orders.

Each time I smiled a weak grin, wondering if I could stay afloat through the new year after all. Then the pain would permeate my arm again, and I'd trust that it was time for this chapter to end. As November rolled into December, I laughed at the irony of my love for cheesy Christmas romantic comedies. As a writer and a baker struggling to make ends meet, I fit the protagonist stereotype to a T. Even my name—Vanderslice—and the name of my dog—Strudel—played into a character who was too cliché to be true.

In these movies, a handsome suitor typically arrives when the failing baker/writer least expects it. He helps her see the ways she's focused too much on her career, resetting her priorities and sweeping her off her feet in a grand gesture of love. The book or the bakery always gets rescued in the end as well.

I watched dozens of the flicks while packaging cookies and loaves to ship to customers across the country. As the storyline played out over and over, I realized I didn't want that kind of ending. The clean-cut conclusion, the happily-ever-after—it was a cop-out. It skimmed over the messy beauty of true community. It failed to acknowledge the value of resting in the unknown while being loved by a community of people, both in person and around the world.

The movie ending offered cake. I wanted bread.

The day after packing up my final loaves and clearing the kitchen of my belongings, I loaded my car with gifts and clothes to drive north to Boston, with Strudel curled up in the backseat. I needed a few weeks to rest and recover, to reimagine what my life might look like in the months ahead. I played the album I'd gotten a few years before—the Advent songs about waiting. I thought about the purpose Companion had served in its short life span.

Bread is, by nature, temporary. It gets eaten or it molds or it goes stale. We must pray for daily bread because bread cannot last forever—it's designed to be consumed. But the bread itself, and the nourishment gleaned from it, is not the sole purpose of the loaf. The waiting, the trusting, the harvesting, the mixing, the shaping, the daily prayer—all of it transforms us slowly, over the course of our lives. It teaches us to hunger for what's to come while keeping us grounded in the moment that we're in.

The closure of Companion was not a sign of failure. In letting go, I got to see the ways the experience shaped me, healed me, and left me hungering for more.

On my way up north, I stopped in Washington, DC, where my younger sister Emma Claire was living. She'd been accepted into the pre-professional training program at the Kirov Academy of Ballet, where instructors fawned over her long, lean limbs. She was preparing to audition for professional ballet companies around the world, eager to launch a career of her own. Having waited to start dance at age sixteen—the same age I'd walked away from ballet—her success was nothing short of a miracle.

"They really think I can make it, Kendall!" Emma Claire told me on the phone a few weeks into her program. "They're giving me extra private lessons, and I get to compete in New York this spring."

"That's great, Em," I responded, holding back my fear that her instructors were giving her false hope. She hadn't been old enough to understand my own experience at Saint Louis Ballet at the time.

"Do you know which variation I'm talking about?" she asked when I'd been quiet for a breath too long.

"No, I don't know that I do," I replied, mustering excitement as best I could.

Over time my concern turned to hope. I understood her underlying drive, and I hoped that through the attention of instructors who saw and valued her skills, she might also find deep satisfaction in moving her body through the choreography.

As I pulled into the circular drive in front of the school, she hugged her friends goodbye. The air outside smelled like it was on the cusp of a solid snow. Emma Claire and her friends giggled about some inside jokes and whined about how long they'd have to go before seeing one another again—three whole weeks.

As she crawled into the car, she leaned over to give me a hug.

"They're the first friends who made me feel like I belong," she said.

We pulled out of the parking lot, her pointe shoes clacking in the backseat. We sat together in contented silence, Strudel snoring loudly. And we drove away.

I ran a small bakery for about two years. In that time, I fed around a thousand people. Maybe I helped them sense, for a moment, God's presence in this world. Or maybe I just brought them a bit of stability in the midst of a turbulent year.

But in the process, I was changed. My needs were met in a manner both miraculous and mundane. And then God asked me to close it down.

There is a time for weeping and a time for celebrating.

A time for fasting and a time for feasting.

A time for singing, a time for dancing.

Sometimes those times are all the same.

It's tempting to look for God at work in big, spectacular ways, to assume that God's movement involves wild answers to prayer. But often God's movement is more subtle. Through the people around us, and through the bread we share, God whispers to us, *I love you. I'm with you. I care.*

This is what it means to pray for daily bread. For daily affirmations of God's presence, provision, and love.

I'm slowly eating my way into understanding that although those bread crumbs might not be satisfying, for this moment, they're enough.

COMPANION BREAD

Like the spelt pita, this bread relies on a prefermentation of the whole wheat flour. It's a high-hydration dough, meaning it has a high ratio of water to flour, and it utilizes a long fermentation to break down the starches in the grain. I call this style of bread "sourdough on training wheels." It's a great way to familiarize yourself with slow, wet dough without giving up the more predictable rhythms of commercial yeast.

½ cup (3 ounces) whole wheat flour
¼ teaspoon instant yeast
1¾ cups (12 ounces) room-temperature water, divided
3 cups (12 ounces) unbleached all-purpose or bread flour
1½ teaspoons kosher salt

1. In a large bowl, mix the whole wheat flour, yeast, and ½ cup water. Let rest for 30 minutes.
2. After the mixture has rested, add the rest of the water, the all-purpose or bread flour, and the salt. Mix by hand until fully incorporated. It might feel soupy at first—that's okay! Cover and let rest for 30 minutes.
3. Stretch and fold the dough in the bowl 4–20 times. Cover again and let rest for 8–12 hours. It will more than double in size.
4. Pour out the dough onto a floured surface, then fold in thirds (like a business letter). Rotate 90 degrees and repeat. Let rest for 10 minutes.
5. Shape the dough into a round loaf or a sandwich loaf and let rest 30 minutes to an hour, until the dough has relaxed. Meanwhile, preheat the oven to 425°F (450°F if using a sandwich pan or a baking tray).
6. Bake for 30–45 minutes, until the crust is brown and the loaf sounds hollow when tapped. Let rest for 30 minutes before serving.

EPILOGUE

Strudel sits perched on the back of the couch, pressed up against the window, looking out over the front patio. A plastic bin filled with poblano white cheddar loaves and a small cashbox teeters on the patio table. One by one, friends swing by to grab their bread and stuff a small bit of money into the box while Strudel howls to say hello.

In the months after Companion closed, Margarita's words about God's provision proved true. I focused my attention on writing, further developing the resources I'd been creating for churches during the height of the pandemic, and I began teaching workshops to help others bake as a form of prayer. I called the business Edible Theology, the name I'd given the email newsletter I'd started a few years before. These new rhythms were easier on my arms and shoulders than repetitively lifting fifty-pound bags of flour and bins of dough, and they provided more stable income as well.

Eventually I was able to buy a house overlooking a park, with a patio perfect for drinking coffee and listening to the Carolina chickadees. In the middle of the home sits a small room with a built-in bookshelf and beadboard paneling from 1947. Most people would consider this room a breakfast nook, but I had other plans. From the minute I saw it, I knew the house was mine. "It's a bread room," I told my real estate agent.

The room now holds a butcher block baker's table and a fifty-gallon drum of flour, as well as a tripod for virtual teaching and recording. Every few weeks, I send an email to friends and former Companion customers: "I'm baking a dozen loaves of bread this week. First twelve to respond get one."

I make just enough to capture the joy but never so much that it brings stress to my day.

Fifteen months after Companion closed down, I sat at my parents' dining table with a group of donors eager to help expand Edible Theology.

"We develop resources that connect the Communion table to the tables we eat at throughout the week," I said before describing our vision for the future.

I'd repeated the line hundreds of times before, but on that night I realized that these were the same words I'd used to describe Companion's mission a few years before. Though Companion was never able to partner with churches in quite the way I'd hoped, its death made possible the launch of the Edible Theology Project—a slower, more stable ministry that reaches further than Companion ever could.

Through Edible Theology, I get to do the things I want to do most. I write, I bake, I research, and I teach. As with the daily supply of manna for the Israelites, I witness God's provision day after day: enough for our needs and, from time to time, a bit extra. But never so much that I cease to experience the delight of praying for daily bread.

Emily—the Durham one—lives down the road from my house, and she comes over a few nights a week so we can cook dinner or watch a movie. Another writer friend, also single, moved to Durham recently, as did Heather, the baker who encouraged me to leave the pop-up job.

From time to time, I take a break in the middle of my workday and meet them for lunch or at the playground across the street. Heather's children take turns going down the slide while she and I catch up on each other's sorrows and joys.

My prayers for marriage and motherhood remain unanswered, though the ache is not as pointed as it once was. I scroll through dating apps, every now and then reaching out to someone interesting. I talk with my doctor about how to prepare my body to support another life, should the opportunity arise. Caring for myself in these ways is a tangible method of holding on to hope. On occasion I allow myself to cry, resting in the tension of many unknowns.

In friendship, in work, and in this house, God has met my deeper needs—providing both cake and bread, which Strudel steals from the kitchen counter.

It might not be satisfying in quite the way I desire, but it's enough.

At least for today.

Appendix

LITURGY FOR BREAD BAKING

Adapted from the prayer liturgy in The Book of Common Prayer

Begin by gathering your supplies:

3 cups white flour (unbleached all-purpose or bread flour will do)
½ cup whole wheat flour
¼ teaspoon yeast (instant or active dry)
1 teaspoon salt (kosher preferred)
1½ cups water, just warm to the touch
1 large mixing bowl
a bowl scraper, if you have one
a light, damp tea towel
your Bible

As you prepare your work space, also prepare your heart and mind.
Slowly breathe and meditate on these words:

Inhale: *My soul finds rest*
Exhale: *in God alone.*[1]

Measure the flour, yeast, and salt into the bowl, and continue meditative breathing. Feel the texture and temperature of each element between your fingers. Give thanks for the community of farmers, millers, and grocers who have brought these ingredients to your kitchen today.

Form a well in the center of the bowl and pause to pray:

Come, let us sing to the LORD;
  let us shout for joy to the Rock of our salvation.
Let us come before his presence with thanksgiving
  and raise a loud shout to him with psalms.
For the LORD is a great God,
  and a great King above all gods.
In his hand are the caverns of the earth,
  and the heights of the hills are his also.
The sea is his, for he made it,
  and his hands have molded dry land.
Come, let us bow down, and bend the knee,
  and kneel before the LORD our Maker.
For he is our God,
and we are the people of his pasture and the sheep of his hand.
  Oh, that today you would hearken to his voice!
PSALM 95:1-7

Pour the water into the center of the well. With your fingers, pull the flour bit by bit into the watery center. Thicken the water slowly, rubbing out dry clumps of flour as they form. Contemplate the feeling of these substances as they transform within your hands.

As the water thickens, continue pulling in flour until the two mixtures are worked into one. Now stop.

The work is not yet done—but it is not all yours to do.

Gently clean the dough off your hands, first with your bowl scraper and then with warm water. Cover the mixture with the damp towel and step away to a silent place. Trust that transformation occurs when your hands and your heart are at rest.

While you wait, read Exodus 16. Pay attention to the ways God encourages the people to wait and trust in the Lord for daily bread.

The word of the Lord.
Thanks be to God.

A song from Mary, the mother of God:

My soul proclaims the greatness of the Lord,
my spirit rejoices in God my Savior;
    for he has looked with favor on his lowly servant.
From this day all generations will call me blessed:
    the Almighty has done great things for me,
    and holy is his Name.
He has mercy on those who fear him
    in every generation.
He has shown the strength of his arm,
    he has scattered the proud in their conceit.
He has cast down the mighty from their thrones,
    and has lifted up the lowly.
He has filled the hungry with good things,
    and the rich he has sent away empty.
He has come to the help of his servant Israel,
    for he has remembered his promise of mercy,
The promise he made to our fathers,
    to Abraham and his children forever.
Glory to the Father, and to the Son, and to the Holy Spirit:
    as it was in the beginning, is now, and will be for ever. Amen.

LUKE 1:46-55

A prayer for guidance:

> *Heavenly Father, in you we live and move and have our being:*
> *We humbly pray you so to guide and govern us by your Holy Spirit,*
> *that in all the cares and occupations of our life we may not forget*
> *you, but may remember that we are ever walking in your sight;*
> *through Jesus Christ our Lord. Amen.*

Now uncover your mixture and grip one side of the dough firmly in your hand. Stretch and fold, and contemplate on the change that has occurred: water flooding and softening the grain, bursting open its tightly wound but untapped strength.

Stretch one side and fold it over the dough. Rotate the bowl 90 degrees and repeat. As you build both elasticity and strength in the bread, pray with each breath:

Inhale: *Oh God* (stretch) *who comes* (fold)
Exhale: *to us* (stretch) *in bread* (fold)

Inhale: *Do not* (stretch) *let us* (fold)
Exhale: *go* (stretch and fold).

Repeat three more times. Cover the dough and let it rest until the same time tomorrow. Remember: transformation occurs, even in our rest.

A benediction before you leave your dough:

> Glory to God whose power, working in us, can do infinitely
> more than we can ask or imagine. Glory to him from generation
> to generation in the Church, and in Christ Jesus for ever and
> ever. Amen.[2]

After the mixture has rested for a day, gather the dough, a bit of flour, a Dutch oven, and a sheet tray or bread pan. As you prepare your workspace, prepare your heart and mind as well.

Slowly breathe and meditate on these words:

Inhale: *Let the words of my mouth and the meditation of my heart*
Exhale: *be acceptable in your sight, O Lord.*[3]

As you flour your counter and pour out your dough, continue meditative breathing. Smell the scent of fermentation, tangy and a little bit sweet. Marvel at the beauty and strength of the mixture, of the bubbles that signal new life and growth.

Now pause to pray:

O gracious light,
pure brightness of the everliving Father in heaven,
O Jesus Christ, holy and blessed!

Now as we come to the setting of the sun,
and our eyes behold the vesper light,
we sing your praises, O God: Father, Son, and Holy Spirit.

You are worthy at all times to be praised by happy voices,
O Son of God, O Giver of Life,
and to be glorified through all the worlds.

Stretch and fold the dough four more times—back and front and side to side. As you do, pray this prayer:

Inhale: *Worship* (stretch) *the Lord* (fold)
Exhale: *in the beauty* (stretch) *of holiness* (fold).

Inhale: *Let the whole* (stretch) *earth tremble* (fold)
Exhale: *before* (stretch) *him* (fold).[4]

Now gently poke your little blob of dough. Allow yourself to revel in just how fun it feels!

Once again, your bread needs rest—the journey from dough to bread must be slow. As the dough rests, it relaxes into its newfound strength. If you push it, it's apt to tear.

While the dough rests, preheat the oven to 450°F. If you have a Dutch oven, preheat it, too. If not, a tray will do.

While you wait, read Matthew 4:1-11. Pay attention to Jesus' choice of words. Remember he is both the Bread of Life and the Word of God.

The word of the Lord.
Thanks be to God.

Also read this song from Simeon, who did not die until he saw Jesus face-to-face:

Lord, you now have set your servant free
    to go in peace as you have promised;
For these eyes of mine have seen the Savior,
    whom you have prepared for all the world to see:
A Light to enlighten the nations,
    and the glory of your people Israel.[5]
Glory to the Father, and to the Son, and to the Holy Spirit:
    as it was in the beginning, is now, and will be for ever. Amen.

Return to your bread, which should be well rested now, and turn it upside down.

Stretch and fold it four more times, then fold it in half and tug to seal the seam and create tension across the surface of the dough. Place the seam side on a piece of parchment for one last rest.

The dough must relax to prepare for this final push, when it will grow with the last bit of energy it can muster.

Now step away to a quiet place. Inhale and exhale with each line of this prayer:

Inhale: *O Lord, show us your mercy,*
Exhale: *and grant us your salvation.*

Inhale: *O Lord, save our nation,*
Exhale: *and guide us in the way of justice and truth.*

Inhale: *Clothe your ministers with righteousness,*
Exhale: *and make your people joyful.*

Inhale: *O Lord, save your people,*
Exhale: *and bless your beloved creation.*

Inhale: *Give peace in our time, O Lord,*
Exhale: *for only in you can we live in safety.*

Inhale: *Let not the needy be forgotten,*
Exhale: *nor the hope of the poor be taken away.*

Inhale: *Create in us clean hearts, O God,*
Exhale: *and take not your Holy Spirit from us.*[6]

Repeat as many times as you must to believe these words are true. (Your bread needs half an hour—it's okay if you do too.)

With a sharp knife, cut a deep slit across the top of the dough. The fermentation needs an outlet for this final push of energy.

Now place the dough in the oven and sprinkle the top with a bit of water. Then watch as the loaf changes before your eyes. Watch the bread grow and burp and relax (about 30 minutes), then pull it out and listen to it sing.

As the coolness meets the heat and the loaf's muscles tighten up once more, the dough will start to crackle.

When the loaf is cooled completely, break it open and share it with people you love.

May the God of hope fill us with all joy and peace in believing through the power of the Holy Spirit. Amen.[7]

GLOSSARY

active dry yeast: see *yeast*

autolyze: a short rest after flour and water have been mixed that allows the flour to hydrate and gluten bonds to form

bran: the outer shell of a wheat kernel containing a high volume of fiber

bread flour: a high-protein flour suitable for making bread, typically made using a hard winter wheat

cold fermentation: see *fermentation*

endosperm: the portion of wheat containing protein and starch; the source of white flour

fermentation: the process of sugars being broken down into alcohols using bacteria and yeast. When bread is made, the carbon dioxide by-product of fermentation is trapped in gluten strands, which raises the dough. This fermentation can take place at room temperature, or it can be slowed down by letting the dough rest at a colder temperature, such as in a refrigerator. The longer, colder fermentation develops more flavor in the dough.

fresh yeast: see *yeast*

germ: the portion of wheat responsible for reproduction and containing a large quantity of fat

gluten: the protein in wheat made up of two amino acids: glutenin and gliadin. As the amino acids form bonds with one another, they create a strong protein network that captures carbon dioxide gas to serve as the backbone of the bread.

high-hydration dough: a dough made with a high ratio of water to flour

instant yeast: see *yeast*

microbiome: the full collection of all microbes, including bacteria, fungi, and viruses, that live on and in a person or thing

pre-fermentation: the preparation of a portion of dough made before the rest of the dough; used to develop nuances of flavor in the bread

proof: also called a rise, this is a rest during which the yeast "proves" it is still alive by growing the dough

semolina: a coarse flour made of the high-protein durum variety of wheat; often used in making pasta

sourdough: a dough leavened using a culture of wild bacteria and yeast rather than commercial yeast

spelt grain: a variety of wheat that is high in protein, with a mellow, nutty flavor

spent grains: the grains left over after the beer-making process. The grains are soaked in water to pull out the starches, which are then mixed with hops and yeast and brewed into beer. The remaining grains are still full of nutrients and flavor.

sprouted-wheat flour: a flour made from wheat that has sprouted.

The kernels have been allowed to begin the process of growing into a plant, then halted, dehydrated, and ground into flour. This process activates enzymes that make the grains more digestible and flavorful.

strudel: a flaky pastry made with many thin layers of dough wrapped around a sweet or savory filling

yeast: In the United States, commercial yeast is typically available from the grocery store in granulated form. Instant (or rapid rise) yeast and active dry yeast are both dehydrated versions of *Saccharomyces cerevisiae*, though the first is ground more finely. I like to think of these types of yeast as being a morning person versus . . . not a morning person. Instant yeast is awake and ready to leaven as soon as it's mixed with flour and water. That means it can typically be mixed directly into the dough. Active dry yeast needs a slower start to its day: a long soak in water and a breakfast of sugar or honey to liven it up before it's ready to get to work in the flour. In a high-hydration, long-fermentation dough, such as the Companion loaf, the slow fermentation makes up for the difference in speed between the two, which means that they can be used interchangeably. Fresh yeast, also known as cake yeast, is *S. cerevisiae* that hasn't been dehydrated or ground into granules. It is prevalent in the United Kingdom but difficult to find in the United States.

DISCUSSION QUESTIONS

You may want to dig deeper into the ideas presented in this book and consider how they intersect with your own story. Feel free to use these questions with a group (preferably over a loaf of bread!) or in your personal reflection.

PART ONE

1. The preface provides background about the history of bread and its impact on culture. What are some of the pivotal stories in your own history with food? How did your family of origin or your spiritual community impact the way you see food?

2. The author describes food as something that can bind communities together as well as something that can cause isolation. How have you experienced both community and isolation as a result of food?

3. In this section, the author writes about her growing awareness of and frustrations with her body. What influences contributed to your awareness of your body as you grew up? In what ways have your feelings about your body changed over the years?

4. In chapter 3, the author talks about the tension between communion and control. What experiences have you had with diet culture and fasting? How have you seen this tension play out?

PART TWO

1. Throughout this section, the author outlines the tension she felt in caring for her physical body as well as her emotional/mental health. What challenges have you experienced in your pursuit of health? In what areas have you experienced healing?

2. In part 2, the author paints a picture of her hunger for community and belonging. When have you felt a longing for connection in your own life? When have you experienced a glimpse of true community?

3. Looking back over her life, the author is able to trace the importance of bread and baking through her story. What threads can you see when you look back at your life? How have you experienced the presence and guidance of God throughout your story?

4. By the end of part 2, we see how the author has begun to find freedom in many areas of her life. In what areas of your own life do you feel free? In what areas are you still seeking freedom?

PART THREE

1. At the opening of part 3, the author draws a connection between yeast and the rhythms of death and life in the human experience. What seasons of death and life have you experienced in your own story? How have you seen death and life intertwined?

2. In chapter 10, we read about bodily knowledge and the way our bodies hold truths that our minds sometimes miss. When has

your body held a date from the past or another truth? What is it like to be reminded of truth in a physical way?

3. Throughout this section, the author struggles to find a clear next step in her life and career. When have you wrestled with what to do next? How did the experience shape you and your relationships?

4. This section closes with a statement about how Communion brings together all types of people, highlighting our need for one another. When have you experienced a meaningful connection over a shared meal, whether inside or outside a church context?

PART FOUR

1. At the beginning of this section, the author tells of her move and her desire to fill her home and table with community. When have you experienced hospitality that led to rich community? How do you feel about inviting people into your home?

2. In chapter 14, the author tells a story of pain that was turned into an invitation. Are there any areas of your life where you've longed for bread but have been given cake instead? In what ways has that longing brought you closer to God?

3. During the lockdown of 2020, many people began baking bread for the first time or returned to the practice. Did you do any baking during that time? What practices or rhythms did you turn to during that season of change and the unknown?

4. At the end of the book, we are reminded of the daily provision and sustenance of bread. How have you seen God provide for you in daily ways? Where might God be inviting you to ask for daily bread?

ACKNOWLEDGMENTS

Every book, like every loaf of bread, is brought to life through community—a network of people who strengthen and flavor it and help it to grow. It is impossible to name everyone who has shaped this book, but there are a handful who deserve my unending thanks.

To my agent, Lisa Jackson, and my team at Tyndale—Kara Leonino, Sarah Atkinson, and Stephanie Rische: thank you for learning with me the dance of when to lean in and when to let go, helping me to unwind and interweave the threads of this story into something cohesive and beautiful.

To the bakers, writers, and scholars whose writing and mentorship have helped me develop my craft, I am indebted to you—especially Peter Reinhart, Maura Kilpatrick and the Sofra team, Lauren Winner, Daniel Train, Katherine Hysmith, and Brian Howell.

To the friends who have supplied me with ice cream and tissues, who have eaten so many loaves of my bread, who have listened to countless voice memos and helped me talk through the same ideas again and again: Emily Ashby, Emily Fiedler, Kaitlyn Schiess, Amanda Windes, I cannot express how much you mean to me. Abby Perry, Kate Watson, and Gabrielle Linnell, bless you for reading draft after draft and continuing to encourage me along the way.

And of course, to my family: words cannot contain the role you've played in shaping my love of food, hospitality, and the Church. I love you.

NOTES

PREFACE
1. William Rubel, *Bread: A Global History* (London: Reaktion Books, 2011), 21.
2. Aaron Bobrow-Strain, *White Bread: A Social History of the Store-Bought Loaf* (Boston: Beacon Press, 2012), 7, 17–33.
3. Dale A. Stirling, "Harvey W. Wiley," *Toxicological Sciences* 67, no. 2 (June 2002): 157–58, https://doi.org/10.1093/toxsci/67.2.157.
4. Bobrow-Strain, *White Bread*, 7, 17–33.
5. Bobrow-Strain, 7, 17–33.
6. Daniel Sack, *Whitebread Protestants: Food and Religion in American Culture* (New York: Palgrave, 2000), 32.
7. *Religious Telescope*, 25 (March 1895): 195.
8. Sack, *Whitebread Protestants*, 36.
9. Sack, 42–43.
10. J. M. Buckley, "The Common Cup or Individual Cups?" *Christian Advocate* 6 (October 1898): 13.
11. John W. Kennedy, "Prepacked Communion Takes Off," *Christianity Today*, April 29, 1996, 58.
12. "Bread," Google Trends, accessed April 22, 2022, https://trends.google.com/trends/explore?date=all&q=bread.
13. Dayna Evans, "Flour Trip," Eater, February 7, 2022, https://www.eater.com/22913142/white-flour-whole-wheat-flour-differences-stone-milled.

CHAPTER 1: ON HUNGER
1. Revelation 22:1-5.
2. "About Us," Mrs Bairds, accessed April 23, 2022, https://www.mrsbairds.com/about-us.

CHAPTER 2: ON BELONGING

1. Thomas Aquinas, *Summa Theologiae*, part 3, question 74, article 3, https://www.newadvent.org/summa/4074.htm.

CHAPTER 3: ON CONTROL

1. Caroline Walker Bynum, *Holy Feast and Holy Fast: The Religious Significance of Food to Medieval Women* (Berkeley: University of California Press, 1987), 4.

CHAPTER 5: ON TRAVEL

1. Rebecca Earle, *The Body of the Conquistador: Food, Race, and the Colonial Experience in Spanish America, 1492–1700* (New York: Cambridge University Press, 2012), 1–18.
2. José de Acosta, *The Natural and Moral History of the Indies*, trans. Edward Grimston, ed. Clements Markham, vol. 2, book 5 (London: Hakluyt Society, 1880), 354–360.
3. Earle, *The Body of the Conquistador*, 92.
4. Willie James Jennings, "'He Became Truly Human': Incarnation, Emancipation, and Authentic Humanity," *Modern Theology* 12, no. 2 (April 1996): 239–55.

CHAPTER 6: ON LONELINESS

1. Sor Juana Inés de la Cruz, "Loa to Divine Narcissus," in *Sor Juana Inés de la Cruz: Selected Writings*, trans. Pamela Kirk Rappaport (New York: Paulist Press, 2005), 69.
2. Sor Juana Inés de la Cruz, "La Respuesta" (par. 28), in *The Answer/La Respuesta, Including a Section of Poems*, trans. Electa Arenal and Amanda Powell (New York: The Feminist Press at The City University of New York, 1994), 75.

CHAPTER 7: ON HEALING

1. Sirach 34:21, 25, NRSV.
2. Bartolemé de Las Casas, *A Short Account of the Destruction of the Indies*, ed. and trans. Nigel Griffin (New York: Penguin Books, 1992).

CHAPTER 8: ON FREEDOM

1. Psalm 34:8.
2. Angel F. Méndez Montoya, *The Theology of Food: Eating and the Eucharist* (UK: Wiley-Blackwell, 2012), 45–46.

CHAPTER 9: ON DEATH

1. Peter Reinhart, "The Art and Craft of Bread," *TED*, July 2008, video, 15:14, https://www.ted.com/talks/peter_reinhart_the_art_and_craft_of_bread?language=en.

CHAPTER 10: ON FRIENDSHIP

1. "The Global Sourdough Project," North Carolina State University Rob Dunn Lab, accessed May 1, 2022, http://robdunnlab.com/projects/sourdough/.

2. Jennifer Brady, "Cooking as Inquiry: A Method to Stir Up Prevailing Ways of Knowing Food, Body, and Identity," *International Journal of Qualitative Methods* 10, no. 4 (December 1, 2011): 321–334, https://doi.org/10.1177/160940691101000402.

CHAPTER 11: ON RESILIENCE
1. Matthew 16:6, EHV.
2. Willie James Jennings, "The Desire of the Church" in *The Community of the Word: Toward an Evangelical Ecclesiology*, ed. Mark Husbands and Daniel J. Treier (Downers Grove, IL: InterVarsity Press, 2005), 248.

CHAPTER 12: ON HOME
1. Ezekiel 37:1-14.

CHAPTER 13: ON HOSPITALITY
1. Tim Daniel Bernard, "A Covenant of Salt," Jewish Theological Seminary, March 27, 2020, https://www.jtsa.edu/a-covenant-of-salt.
2. Hermann Eising, *Theological Dictionary of the Old Testament*, vol. IV, ed. G. Johannes Botterweck and Helmer Ringgren, trans. David E. Green (Grand Rapids, MI: Eerdmans, 1980), 331–333.
3. Robert Farrar Capon, *The Supper of the Lamb: A Culinary Reflection* (New York: Doubleday, 1969), 189.
4. Capon, *The Supper of the Lamb*, 118.
5. Capon, 121.

CHAPTER 14: ON LONGING
1. Psalm 80:6.
2. Malcolm Guite, "LXXX Qui Regis Israel" in "The Bread of Tears: A Response to Psalm 80," *Malcolm Guite* (blog), January 26, 2021, https://malcolmguite.wordpress.com/2021/01/26/the-bread-of-tears-a-response-to-psalm-80/.
3. The Porter's Gate, "Your Labor Is Not in Vain," *Work Songs: The Porter's Gate Worship Project*, released October 6, 2017, https://www.theportersgate.com/.
4. The Porter's Gate, "In the Fields of the Lord," *Work Songs*.

CHAPTER 15: ON CONTENTMENT
1. 2 Kings 2:19-22, NIV.
2. *Didache*, also known as "The Teaching of the Twelve Apostles," chapter 9.

CHAPTER 16: ON HOPE
1. M. K. Gandhi, *Village Swaraj*, compiled by H. M. Vyas, (Ahmedabad, India: Navajivan Trust, 1962), https://www.mkgandhi.org/ebks/village_swaraj.pdf.
2. Kenneth Pletcher, "Salt March," *Encyclopedia Britannica*, June 26, 2019, https://www.britannica.com/event/Salt-March.

3. Wim Hordijk, "From Salt to Salary: Linguists Take a Page from Science," NPR, *Cosmos & Culture*, November 8, 2014, https://www.npr.org/sections/13.7/2014 /11/08/362478685/from-salt-to-salary-linguists-take-a-page-from-science#:~ :text=Being%20so%20valuable%2C%20soldiers%20in,as%20the%20word %20%22salary.%22.

APPENDIX: LITURGY FOR BREAD BAKING

1. Psalm 62:1.
2. Ephesians 3:20-21.
3. Psalm 19:14.
4. Psalm 96:9.
5. Luke 2:29-32.
6. Psalm 51:10-11.
7. Romans 15:13.

ABOUT THE AUTHOR

KENDALL VANDERSLICE is a baker, writer, and speaker, as well as the founder of the Edible Theology Project, a ministry that connects the Communion table to the kitchen table. She is a graduate of Wheaton College (BA anthropology), Boston University (MLA gastronomy), and Duke Divinity School (master of theological studies). Her bylines include *Christianity Today*, *Bitter Southerner*, *Christian Century*, *Religion News Service*, and *Faith and Leadership*. She is the author of *We Will Feast* (Eerdmans, 2019). Kendall lives (with her big-eared beagle named Strudel) in Durham, North Carolina, where she teaches workshops on bread baking as a spiritual practice. Visit her online at kendallvanderslice.com.

edible theology

Find delight, rest, and connection in the kitchen and at the table.

Learn more at **edibletheology.com**